The Woman Who Finds Herself

Jeanie Matthews Wooten

Avant-garde Books, LLC
Spiritual Division
Post Office Box 566
Mableton, Georgia 30126
www.avantgardebooks.net

The Woman Who Finds Herself

Scriptures are taken from the King James Version of
the Holy Bible.

ISBN: 978-1-946753-13-7

For additional copies of this book, please contact:

Wooten Ministries
2400 Walker Circle
Sarasota, Florida 34234
Phone: (941) 366-2943

This book is dedicated to all the women in the world, and to the bloodline of the Lamar and Matthews Families

Table of Contents

Introduction
The Woman Who Finds Herself

It is important for everyone, especially women, to know themselves. In other words, know who you are, not who someone says you are. Coming from a spiritual perspective, the woman who finds herself needs to know who they are in Christ Jesus. In the old testament of the Holy Bible, women were treated as property, not counted; they had no rights.

Men have been taught that they are the head of the woman. "For the husband is the head of the wife, even as Christ is the head of the church: and he is the savior of the body." (Ephesians 5:23)

Does this mean that the woman should be treated as a second-class citizen? A woman told me that she had been "used and abused", but she finally found peace. Some of us have read in the Bible about the women who have done outstanding things. Also, there are thousands of notable, nationally known women who have done marvelous, great things in their lives to help their families, their community, their state, and their country. Many are alive; and some are deceased.

In addition to the above women, you will read about a few women who might not be known nationally. These are women whom I know or have known personally. All of us have our faults or shortcomings, but I have put emphasis on the positive, good deeds of these women.

Society has a standard of living for women and a standard for men. The Holy Bible is written for all believers in Christ Jesus to live by. "There is neither Jew nor Greek, there is neither bond nor free, there is neither male nor female; for ye are all one in Christ Jesus." (Galatians 3:28)

There are some folk who refuse to acknowledge me as a minister, but have I let that stop me from preaching the gospel or from doing the work of an evangelist? I say nay because I know who anointed me to do so.

Sometimes women are put down, harassed, criticized, and rejected in so many ways that they don't know who they are, or where they belong. These insulting, degrading behaviors might occur in the home, on the job, in the church, or elsewhere. These behaviors don't always come from males, but by women who are jealous and covetous. Their motive is to destroy you because they are inferior.

If the woman is not careful, she will fall into satan's snares, then low self-esteem might develop, as well as anger and depression. If someone calls you fat, skinny, stupid, crazy, ugly, and so forth, don't allow that negativity to corrupt your mind.

Every woman should want to feel good about herself because if she doesn't, this could be a hindering block to prevent her from reaching her potential or goal. As I said before, we study and write about the good and bad behavior regarding the women in the Bible. Do we ever think about the women who are around us?

There are thousands of intelligent, brilliant, gorgeous, wise women to whom we talk often; with whom we go to church; and with whom we work on our jobs, yet we don't tell the world about them. I realize that some women who "don't" work behind the scenes, they get some recognition.

All women do not have the same gifts and talents, and if we spend too much time trying to be like someone else, we might miss out on what God wants us to become. In order to find out who you are spiritually, you must find yourself in the word of God and make corrections where it is needed. Sometimes we spend too much time finding other's faults.

By reading the life stories of a few women, their testimonies, their calling, their gifts and talents, and their accomplishments, hopefully this will be an incentive for you to know the sky is the limit. In addition, the objective for writing this book is to encourage, to uplift, to educate the Christian woman, the married woman, the single woman, the divorcee, the employee, the retiree, and others. We can conclude that this book is also written to educate, to convict the minds of those who look upon women only as domestic workers, and as sex objects or as property.

If we have the spirit of the Lord abiding in us, we will seek His face concerning whatever decisions we make, then instead of confusion or frustration, the fruit of the spirit will remain — love, joy, peace...

A Special Tribute

There are thousands of women who are nationally known and have blazed the trail for women who are too afraid to explore and discover their hidden gifts and talents. Some of these pioneers are deceased and some are still alive.

From the beginning of this world's existence, countless extraordinary women with brilliant minds have done remarkable, outstanding work. Remember, women were not allowed to vote until 1920.

I personally commend these dignitaries whether they are African-Americans, Hispanics, Asian American, Indians Caucasians or others because through faith and perseverance, despite struggles, oppositions, and so forth, they didn't quit—they made it to a higher dimension.

It should be understood that every woman may not have the abilities that these women have but covet the best gift or talent that the Lord has given you. The following is a list of only a few among thousands whose level of work surpasses the average.

Shirley Chisholm (1924 – 2005), the first black woman ever elected to congress, declared her candidacy for the Democratic nomination for president. She wrote of her unsuccessful bid. She continued to speak out for the rights of women, people of color, and the poor. (United States Postal Service)

Hillary Clinton, the first female major party presidential nominee, first lady — married to former President Bill Clinton, former Secretary of State, former senator, broke barriers and much more.

Whoopi Goldberg, versatile actress and entertainer, a great television talk show leader having incredible insight, wisdom, and knowledge. "The View" women are highly intelligent and interesting.

Sarah Greene, former president and CEO of the National Head Start Association.

Michelle Obama, former first black lady of the United States married to former President Barack Obama, by having a genius mind, introduced new innovations.

Rosa Parks (1913 – 2005), refused to give up her seat on a bus to a white man. She became a civil rights icon. (Life Magazine: 100 Women Who Changed the World, 2015)

Janet Reno (1938 – 2016), first female attorney general of the United States. She was a native of Florida.

Frances Swaggert, spiritual teacher on SBN has a show, "Frances and Friends" that allows callers to get spiritual advice and guidance; ask questions; and make comments. (Jimmy Swaggert Ministries)

Harriet Tubman (1822 – 1913), a former slave who risked her life to free thousands of slaves through the underground railroad. (Life Magazine: 100 Women Who Changed the World, 2015)

Barbara Walters, the first woman morning show cohost; first woman network news co-anchor; master interviewer of world leaders and celebrities; correspondent and cohost of ABC's 20/20 for 25 years. (AARP Magazine, 2014).

Oprah Winfrey, hosted the Oprah Winfrey Show for 25 seasons; produces films, great actress, publishes a monthly magazine, co-written books, cofounder of the Oxygen Network, and much more. (Life Magazine: 100 Women Who Changed the World, 2015)

Chapter One
Jeanie's Wise Sayings

"For the LORD giveth wisdom:
out of his mouth cometh
knowledge and
understanding"
(Proverbs 2:6)

Chapter One
Jeanie's Wise Sayings

A woman who visits or calls once a year with encouraging words is a closer friend than one who calls every day with derogatory remarks.

The woman with the loud mouth can be heard down the street, and the man she wants will continue to sleep.

The woman who puts a stumbling block in her sister's way is like a dog who bites its owner.

A woman who has no originality but copies what others do is like a lazy duck who refuses to quack.

A woman who becomes complacent and never seeks to move up higher is like a fishing rod that sits by the lake.

The woman who obeys the Lord is blessed above the one who strives to emulate.

The woman who expresses her anger will soon forget it as opposed to the one who smiles and carries the anger in her heart.

I would rather see an honest woman wearing a short, blue dress than to see a woman with an evil heart wearing a long, white garment.

The prostitute who walks the street is more truthful than the woman who says, "I'll date you, but it's going to cost you."

The woman who admits I don't know is more humble than the one who steals and exalts herself.

The woman who criticizes and has a solution is better than a donating fault finder.

Beware of a woman with an evil heart. She will do what she thinks you will dislike.

The jealous heart will watch what you do, then competes to become superior to you.

To cover up her covetousness, a woman will buy what you buy, then accuse you of jealousy.

The woman who finds fault in your talents and your gifts is more likely trying to get the same.

A woman who shouts, "I love you," in every conversation is like a dog who continually barks, but will not bite.

Avoid a troublemaker, for she has no limit to the depth of her wickedness.

A woman who tries to disguise her true feelings is like a poisonous snake hiding in the grass.

An enemy gets angry when her evil deeds are revealed, then blame is switched.

If you want to send a message, a female meddler will save you the energy.

The woman with a double mind will smile in your face while stabbing you in your back.

The motives of a woman who gives to gain control are like a rooster in the hen house.

When a woman has bullhorns, her aggressive behavior is like a lion in the jungle.

A trickster falls into the traps she sets for others.

To justify jealousy and covetousness is like a liar whose feet are stuck in the mud.

The woman who acts out her lies is the same as one who betrays the innocent.

To live as a wife for forty years in sadness is worse than a marriage of two weeks with joy.

When a woman's wicked deeds are uncovered, she will slander your name.

An inferior woman wants you to tell her all you know so she can get the praise.

A trickster will do what you do, then accuse you of stealing from her.

If love is pure, hypocrisy can't be found.

Chapter Two
Becoming a Holy Woman

"When we do the best we can, we never know what miracle is wrought in our life, or in the life of another."—Helen Keller

Chapter Two
Becoming a Holy Woman

Step 1: Hear the Gospel

"And Jesus answered him, the first of all the commandments is Hear, O Israel: The Lord our God is one Lord." (Saint Mark 12:29)

"How then shall they call on him in whom they have not believed? And how shall they believe in him of whom they have not heard? And, how shall they hear without a preacher?" (Romans 10:14)

"So then faith cometh by hearing, and hearing by the word of God." (Romans 10:17)

Step 2: Believe the Gospel

"That if thou shalt confess with thy mouth the Lord Jesus, and shalt believe in thine heart that God hath raised him from the dead, thou shalt be saved." (Romans 10:9)

"For by grace are ye saved through faith; and that not for yourselves: it is the gift of God." (Ephesians 2: 8)

"For I am not ashamed of the gospel of Christ: for it is the power of God unto salvation to everyone that believeth: To the Jew first, and also to the Greek." (Romans 1:16)

"Now after that John was put in prison. Jesus came into Galilee, preaching the gospel of the kingdom of God and saying, the time is fulfilled, and the Kingdom of God is at hand: repent ye, and believe the gospel." (Saint Mark 1:14-15)

Step 3: Repent and Confess

"The sacrifices of God are a broken spirit; a broken and a contrite heart, O God, thou wilt not despise." (Psalm 51:17)

"In those days came John the Baptist, preaching in the wilderness of Judaea, and saying, Repent ye: for the kingdom of heaven is at hand." (Matthew 3:1-2)

 "Then Peter said unto them, repent, and be baptized every one of you in the name of Jesus Christ for the remission of sins, and ye shall receive the gift of the Holy Ghost." (Acts 2:38)

"That if thou shalt confess with thy mouth the Lord Jesus, and shalt believe in thine heart that God hath raised him from the dead, thou shalt be saved." (Romans 10:9)

"For with the heart man believeth unto righteousness; and with the mouth confession is made unto salvation." (Romans 10:10)

"If we confess our sins, he is faithful and just to forgive us our sins, and to cleanse us from all unrighteousness." (I John 1:9)

"He that covereth his sins shall not prosper: but who confesseth and forsaketh them shall have mercy." (Proverbs 28:13)

"I acknowledged my sin unto thee, and mine iniquity have I not hid. I said, I will confess my transgressions unto the Lord; and thou forgavest the iniquity of my sin." (Psalm 32:5)

Step 4: Be Baptized

"Know ye not, that so many of us were baptized unto Jesus Christ were baptized unto his death? Therefore, we are buried with him by baptism unto death that like as Christ was raised up from the dead by glory of the Father, even so we also should walk in newness of life." (Romans 6:3-4)

"Now when all the people were baptized, it came to pass that Jesus also being baptized, and praying, the heaven was opened, and the Holy Ghost descended in a bodily shape like a dove upon him, and a voice came from heaven which said, Thou art my beloved Son; in thee I am well pleased." (Saint Luke 3:21-22)

"And as they went on their way, they came unto a certain water: and the eunuch said, see, here is water; what doth hinder me to be baptized? And they went down both into the water, both Philip and the eunuch; and he baptized him." (Acts 8:36-38)

Step 5: Receive the Holy Spirit

"But ye are not in the flesh, but in the Spirit, if so be that the Spirit of God dwell in you. Now if any man has not the Spirit of Christ, he is none of his." (Romans 8:9)

"If ye then, being evil, know how to give good gifts to your children: how much more shall your heavenly Father give the Holy Spirit to them that ask him?" (Saint Luke 11: 13)

"Be ye shall receive power, after that the Holy Ghost is come upon you: and ye shall be witnesses unto me both in Jerusalem, and in all Judea, and in Samaria, and unto the uttermost part of the earth." (Acts 1:8)

"Hereby know we that we dwell in him, and he in us, because he hath given us of his Spirit." (I John 4:13)

"And it came to pass that while Apollos was at Corinth, Paul having passed through the upper coasts came to Ephesus: and finding certain disciples, He said unto them, Have ye received the Holy Ghost since ye believe? And they said unto him, we have not so much as heard whether there be any Holy Ghost." (Acts 19:1-2)

"When they heard this, they were baptized in the name of the Lord Jesus. And when Paul had laid his hands upon them, the Holy Ghost came on them; and they spake with tongues and prophesied." (Acts 19:5-6)

"Then remembered I (Peter) the word of the Lord, how that he said, John indeed baptized with water, but ye shall be baptized with the Holy Ghost." (Acts 11:16)

Step 6: Learn the Word

"Come unto me, all ye that labor and are heavy laden, and I will give you rest. Take my yoke upon you and learn of me; for I am meek and lowly in heart: and ye shall find rest unto your souls. For my yoke is easy, and my burden is light." (Saint Matthew 11:28-30)

"Wherewithal shall a young man cleanse his way? By taking heed thereto according to thy word." (Psalm 119:9)

"Now ye are clean through the Word which I have spoken unto you." (Saint John 15: 3)

"Being born again, not of corruptible seed, but of incorruptible, by the word of God, which liveth and abideth forever." (I Peter 1:23)

"Sanctify them through thy truth: Thy Word is truth." (Saint John 17:17)

Step 7: Live by Every Word of God

"Man shall not live by bread alone, but by every word that proceedeth out of the mouth of God." (Saint Matthew 4:4)

"My little children, let us not love in word, neither in tongue; but indeed, and in truth." (I John 3:18)

"If ye keep my commandments, ye shall abide in my love; even as I have kept my Father's commandments and abide in his love." (Saint John 15:10)

Chapter Three
The Barren Women

"A woman is a like a tea bag—
you can't tell how strong she is
until you put her in hot water."
—Eleanor Roosevelt

Chapter Three
The Barren Women

In this chapter, you will read about some women who were barren, but the Lord decreed that they would bear a child. It had been prophesized that their children would become great men and women of God. Nothing is impossible with God!

The women who remained barren have a work to do: "The Lord maketh the barren woman to keep house, and to be a joyful mother of children." (Psalm 113:9)

Sarai (Sarah)

Sarah was the wife of Abraham and she was barren while in her old age. The Lord said to Abraham that Sarah would bare him a son and his name would be called Isaac, and he was going to establish an everlasting covenant with him. "Then Abraham fell upon his face, and laughed, and said in his heart, shall a child be born unto him that is a hundred years old? And, shall Sarah that is ninety years old, bear?" (Genesis 17:17)

Sarah still thought that she could not bear a biological child, so she told her husband to go into her handmaid, Hagar, so she could bear a son for her. Hagar bore Abraham a son and called his name

Ishmael. God's plan for Ishmael was not the son that he would establish his covenant with.

Angels visited Abraham and reminded him that Sarah, his wife shall bear a son. Sarah was in the tent and heard it, and she laughed in her heart and said, "After I am waxed old shall I have pleasure, my lord being old also?" (Genesis 18:12)

Sarah conceived as the Lord said she would and bore Abraham a son and called his name Isaac. Sarah was a hundred twenty-seven years old when she died. Her son became the father of Esau and Jacob. His wife's name was Rebekah. Jacob, their youngest son, became the father of the twelve tribes of Israel through his wives, Leah and Rachael, and their handmaidens. Jesus, our Savior, came through the lineage of Judah, Leah's fourth son. All nations are blessed through Abraham, Isaac, and Jacob.

The Wife of Manoah

There was a man name Manoah from the tribe of Dan whose wife had no child. "The angel of the Lord appeared unto the woman, and said unto her, "Behold now, thou art barren, and bearest not: but thou shalt conceive, and bear a son." (Judges 13:3)

This woman was instructed as to what to drink and eat: drink no wine or strong drink, and to eat nothing unclean. The angel also described certain things about the child she was going to bear: He will be a Nazarite from the womb; no razor will come upon his head. This child's mission from the Lord was to deliver Israel out of the hand of the Philistines. Manoah's wife shared with her husband what the angel had said to her.

The angel's words came true for Manoah's wife. She conceived and bore a son who was called Samson. Samson became a judge of Israel. The Lord blessed him to have extraordinary strength. Israel was under the authority of the Philistines. However, Samson destroyed many of them.

Later, Samson married a woman named Delilah who was offered money to betray him. He told her the secret of where his strength came. When she told his enemies, he was captured and blinded, and his hair was cut off. In the end, Samson killed many Philistines as well as himself.

The Shunamite Woman

There was a Shunamite woman who had no child, and her husband was old. Elisha, the prophet said unto her, "About this season, according to the time of life, thou shalt embrace a son." (II Kings 4:14-37)

Later, the woman conceived and bore a son at the time of season just like the prophet had told her. After the child was grown, he complained about his head, for he was out in the field with his father and the reapers. The Shunamite's son died. However, the woman had faith in the man of God, so she laid her son on the prophet's bed.

The Lord had not told the man of God what had happened to the woman's son. She reminded the man of God that she didn't want him to lie to her. She was wondering why God would bless her with a child, but then take him away from her.

Elisha, the prophet, went up and lay upon the child, and put his mouth upon his mouth, and his eyes upon his eyes, and his hands upon his hands. He stretched himself upon the child; and the flesh of the child waxed warm. The child sneezed seven times and his eyes opened.

When you show kindness to anyone, especially to a man or woman of God, the Lord will bless you. Saint Mark 9:41 says, "For whosoever shall give you a cup of water to drink in my name, because ye belong to Christ, verily I say unto you, he shall not lose his reward."

Mary, the mother of Jesus

Mary was a virgin who was highly favored by God to be the mother of our Lord and Savior, Jesus Christ. She did not know how this could be because she did not know a man. Mary was espoused to a man whose name was Joseph. "The angel of the

Lord appeared unto him in a dream, saying, Joseph, thou son of David, fear not to take unto thee Mary thy wife: for that which is conceived in her is of the Holy ghost" (Saint Matthew 1:20).

There was much prophecy regarding the coming of Christ. The name JESUS was given before he was born, and that he would come to save his people from their sins. Saint Luke 1:35 says that his child shall be called the Son of God.

"Mary brought forth her first-born son and wrapped him in swaddling clothes and laid him in a manger" (Saint Luke 2:7). As Jesus grew, Mary knew she had a son sent from God, so she followed him, even when he hung on the cross at Calvary, and she was in the upper room in prayer before the Holy Ghost came.

Chapter Four
Prayers Answered

"Be careful for nothing; but in everything by prayer and supplication with thanksgiving let your requests be made known unto God. And the peace of God, which passeth all understanding, shall keep your hearts and minds through Christ Jesus."
(Philippians 4:6-7)

Chapter Four
Prayers Answered

"There are three things that are never satisfied, yea, four things say not, it is enough: The grave; and the barren womb: the earth that is not filled with water; and the fire that saith not, it is enough" (Proverbs 30:15-16)

In this chapter, you will read about some women who never birth a child, and through prayer, the Lord blessed and opened their wombs: and some women who had birth a child or children, then they ceased from bearing, but through prayer, they were able to bear again.

Rachel

Rachel was barren until the Lord remembered her, and opened up her womb, and took away her reproach – God hearkened to her. Rachel was the youngest daughter of Laban, the son of Nahor. His eldest daughter was named Leah.

When Jacob saw Rachel at the well, he fell in love with her. Jacob agreed to work for Laban seven years so that he could marry her. It was a custom that the eldest daughter should marry first, so Leah served her week as Jacob's wife, then Rachel became his wife also, though he worked another seven years.

Leah began to bear children for Jacob and Rachel envied her, and said unto Jacob, "Give me children, or else I die." (Genesis 30:1). Jacob got angry and said, "Am I in God's stead, who hath withheld from thee the fruit of the womb?" (Genesis 30:2)

Both sisters had their handmaids to bear children for them. "Rachel conceived, and bare a son; and said, God hath taken away my reproach: And she called his name Joseph, and said, The Lord shall add to me another son" (Genesis. 30:23-34).

Rachel conceived again and when she was in hard labor with Benoni, she died. Jacob called his son Benjamin. Joseph was a special child who was loved by God, and by his father. However, he was hated by his brothers. He was a dreamer and God gave him the gift of interpreting dreams. Joseph was made ruler over Egypt.

Eventually, Joseph became the governor over the land. He went through trials such as, placed in prison, lied on, and much more, but the Lord was always with him. He blessed his family and all the people during the time of a famine.

Rebekah

"And Isaac entreated the Lord for his wife, because she was barren: and the Lord was entreated of him, and Rebekah his wife conceived" (Genesis 25:21). Rebekah had twins whose names were Esau and Jacob. Jacob asked Esau to sell him his birthright. "He sold his birthright unto Jacob" (Genesis 25:33). "Then Jacob gave Esau bread and pottage of lentils; and he did eat and drink, and rose up, and went his way; thus, Esau despised his birthright" (Genesis 25:34).

Jacob became the father of the twelve tribes of Israel.

Hannah

Hannah's husband was named Elkanah and he loved her very much although she was barren until the Lord opened her womb. Elkanah had another wife whose name was Peninnah and she had children. Peninnah poked fun at Hannah and she would weep because her heart was grieved. One day, Hannah began to pray to the Lord for a male child. She promised that if he answered this request, she would give the child back to him all the days of his life.

During the time Hannah was praying, her voice was not heard, so Eli the priest thought she was drunk. After the priest told her that God had answered her prayer, she began to feel better – she was no longer sad, and she could eat. "Hannah conceived, that she bore a son, and called his name Samuel, saying, Because I have asked him of the Lord" (1 Samuel 1:20). Hannah kept her word because she brought the child unto the house of the Lord to Eli after she had weaned Samuel.

When Hannah and her husband came up to offer their sacrifices, they would see Samuel. One time she made him a little coat. Because Hannah had loaned Samuel unto the Lord; Eli prayed for the Lord to bless Elkannah and Hannah to bare more children. Hannah had three more sons and two daughters.

Samuel was called to serve the Lord from a child, and as he grew, he served as a priest and as a prophet.

Elizabeth

Elizabeth was of the daughters of Aaron, the priest. Her husband's name was Zechariah and he was a priest. They were both righteous. "And they had no child, because Elizabeth was barren, and they both were now well stricken in years" (Saint Luke 1:7). An angel appeared unto Zechariah and said the

Lord has heard his prayer and Elizabeth was going to bear him a son and he shall be named John. Zechariah thought the Lord had forgotten his prayer. He received much prophecy about this unborn child. One of the most important prophecies is that the child will be filled with the holy ghost from his mother's womb.

Later, Elizabeth conceived just like the angel said she would. At the time Elizabeth was about six months pregnant, Virgin Mary, her cousin, went to Zechariah's house, and when she spoke to Elizabeth, "the babe leaped in her womb: and Elizabeth was filled with the Holy Ghost." (Saint Luke 1:41)

When Elizabeth's baby was born, cousins and neighbors wanted to name him Zechariah, but Elizabeth said no, his name shall be called John. His father wrote on a pad that his name shall be called John.

"And thou child, shalt be called the prophet of the Highest; For thou shalt go before the face of the Lord to prepare his way; to give knowledge of salvation unto his people by the remission of their sins." (Saint Luke 1:76-77)

John baptized with water in Bethabara beyond Jordan. He even baptized Jesus. "For I say unto you, among those that are born of women there is not a greater prophet than John, the Baptist: but he that is least in the kingdom of God is greater than he." (Saint Luke 7:28)

Jeana Lynn Graham

Jeana had ceased from bearing a child for over 20 years when she and her husband decided that they wanted a baby boy. Her two daughters, Jenae and Kendra, were both attending universities at that time. Through prayer God opened her womb again. I, the writer of this book, laid hands on my daughter and prayed. I received much prophecy about the coming of this child. I saw in the spirit that she would conceive and have a son. I saw her sitting in a rocking chair holding a baby.

My daughter received more prophecy from the late, Bishop Wesley Tunstall. He told her that she would have a boy child and he did not know what the Lord had already told me. The little miracle son is named Harold Josiah (JoJo). He is seven years old now and he surprises everyone with what he says and does. He learned how to do many things at an early age such as walking, talking, being potty trained, and excelling in sports. I took him to church one night, and when he heard the preacher, he told me he wanted to preach.

From a child, Jeana has known the scriptures. She could memorize chapters in the Bible. "Train up a child in the way he should go; and when he is old, he will not depart from it." (Proverbs 22:6). She spent most of her early childhood in Fort Lauderdale,

Florida then I moved to Sarasota, Florida in obedience to the Lord.

During a church service in Fort Lauderdale, Jeana gave the preacher her hand and said she wanted to join the church. She was later baptized. She was only about five or six years old. She had not been coerced to do that.

She always used her brilliant mind in so many ways. She was determined to earn a college degree. She didn't allow marriage, children, or anything else to hinder her from getting a higher education. She seemingly enjoys helping children — sometimes with programs at church and at school; and teaching vacation Bible school.

Regarding her work career, she has had experiences as a teacher with Head Start in Manatee County and Child Care Connection in Broward County. She has served as an elementary school teacher with Manatee and Broward counties (Florida), and several years as a high school teacher having administrative duties in Fort Lauderdale, Florida.

I will only name a few of her awards and accomplishments: Teacher of the Year for James Tillman Elementary; Teacher of the Year from the People's Appreciation Award Banquet; Hometown Hero in the Bradenton Herald Newspaper; and Chairperson Black History Month.

Jeana Lynn did so many things to motivate her students to become interested in learning. I am so grateful that the Lord blesses her to drive to Sarasota and serve as mistress of ceremony for the Wooten's Annual Concerts.

I gave Jeana her name because during the time I was pregnant with the oldest child, my grandmother-in-law would always call me Jeana, not Jeanie. I told my husband that if this baby is a girl, I want to name her Jeana. However, our first baby was a boy, but our second was a girl and we named her Jeana.

In so many ways, Jeana's life parallels with my life. Our lives have a lot in common, just to name a few: (1) I was born on Sunday and Jeana was born on Sunday; (2) I have three biological children and Jeana has three, too; (3) I had one child born in February and fifteen months later, Jeana was born. Jeana had one child born in February and fifteen months later, she had a child born in July; (4) I earned more than a bachelor's degree, and Jeana earned more than a bachelor's degree; (5) My first professional job was teaching and Jeana's first professional job was teaching; and (6) I am creative and know how to organize and so does Jeana in a greater superb way.

During our lifetime, we have made choices that were not directed by the Lord, especially during our young adult life, but we are both "chosen" vessels for the Lord. This means that we should be obedient to

God. For instance, if a man tells the Lord he is looking for a wife, and the Lord chooses one of us to be his wife, we obey. If the husband decides not to transform his mind and ways from the world, the Lord might move him out of our life, and to say to me or Jeana, I have another mate for you. I explained that because we cannot make choices like traditional women do.

I was married to one husband for about 12 years and was married to another for about five years. Jeana was married to one husband for five years and was married to another for 12 years.

On March 20, 1999, the Lord said, "Jeana is being trained for the work I have called her to do. She will work with children, teenagers, and adults. She is versatile just like you, Jeanie."

Chapter Five
Women as Mothers

"I believe the choice to become a mother is the choice to become one of the greatest spiritual teachers there is." – Oprah Winfrey

Chapter Five
Women as Mothers

Mother is a name given by the Lord God. Eve was called mother. She was the first mother. "And Adam called his wife's name Eve because she was the mother of all living." (Genesis 3:20)

Sarah became the mother of many nations. "And God said unto Abraham, as for Sarai thy wife, thou shalt not call her name Sarai; but Sarah shall her name be. And I will bless her and give thee a son also of her; yea, I will bless her, and she shall be a mother of nations; kings of people shall be of her." (Genesis 17:15-16)

On January 1, 2004, the Lord said, "Jeanie, I am raising you up. Your official name is Mother Wooten at your church even if some reject your name is Mother Wooten." Some members were already calling me Mother Wooten. The name Mother carries a distinct title; a spiritual title that some think very little of. According to I Timothy 5:2, the elder women should be treated as mothers.

Beside spiritual mothers, there are many types of mothers such as biological mothers, grandmothers, stepmothers, mothers-in-law, godmothers, mothers by adoption, surrogate mothers, as so forth.

The word, mother, has reference to a female parent. Regardless to the age of her child, a real mother will always be mom — maybe in different roles according to the child's age; but the mother's love is exemplified. Mothers should train, teach, and protect their children, but we cannot over protect them. If we do, they will not develop or grow into full adult maturity. In all their ways, our children should mature. Jesus is a jealous God. We cannot worship another.

Mothers should live a holy life before our children if we expect them to become holy one day. Here is an example of a mother who thought she was saying what was right for her sons because she loved them so much. The mother of James and John, the sons of Zebedee, asked Jesus to "grant that these my two sons may sit, the one on the right hand, the other on the left, in thy kingdom." (Saint Matthew 20:21) Jesus answered and said, "Ye know not what ye ask. Are ye able to drink of the cup that I shall drink of, and to be baptize with the baptism that I am baptized with?" (Saint Matthew 20:22)

The scriptures speak of many caring mothers for instance, when Moses was a baby and was rescued out of the water, Pharaoh's daughter told the maid to call Jochebed, the child's mother to nurse it for her. She paid her wages. Moses became the son of Pharaoh's daughter. (Exodus 1:9)

Another example of a mother's love is when a woman who was a Greek, a Syrophenician, had a young daughter who had an unclean spirit. She brought the child to Jesus for him to cast out the devil in her. When the mother returned home, the devil was gone out of her daughter. In 1 Kings 17:17-24, there was a widow woman who had a son who fell so sick that no breath was in his body.

Elijah took the child out of her bosom and prayed that the Lord let the child's soul come into him again. When Elijah delivered the child alive unto his mother, the widow woman said, "Now, by this I know that thou art a man of God, and that the word of the Lord in thy mouth is truth."

Georgia Lamar Matthews (Tindal)
A Caring Mother

Georgia was one of the daughters of the late Turner and Josie Lamar. She was a petite, wise and witty person. Her laughter could draw a crowd. Georgia told her children that her mother died when she was a teenager. At the age of eighteen, she married Grady Matthews on April 10, 1926. They moved from Sylvester, Georgia to Weirsdale, Florida.

Georgia bore thirteen children. The youngest child, whose name was Diane, died as a baby, so she and Grady raised twelve children to adulthood. Only four of these children are alive today. All her sons and daughters were academically smart. However, her daughter, Georgia was the first child to attend college; and Pearl was the first to earn a bachelor's degree.

Georgia was a faithful member of Stanton First Baptist Church where she sang in the choir, read her Bible, and wore beautiful clothes and shoes of all colors.

Georgia had at least a six-grade education. She could read and write well. She didn't work outside the home. She was home when her children went to school, when they came home for lunch, and when they came home when school was out. She was her husband's secretary/bookkeeper as he worked as a citrus foreman. She also sewed by hand (no machine) in making skirts, slips, quilts, and much more. She kept a garden that consisted of tomatoes, corn, okra, sugar cane, greens and so forth. She planted beautiful flowers around the house.

Georgia enjoyed supporting her children in their church functions and in their school activities. She taught her girls how to cook, wash clothes, clean and iron. Her girls will never forget some of her favorite words: "Y'all guls [sic] better listen to me, cause I'm the best friend you got." Some other words were: "Don't cut your hair – it is your glory."

After thirty-five years of marriage, death separated Grady and Georgia. Later, she married Deacon Romie Tindal. When her health declined, she lived with several daughters until her death on October 14, 1971 in Fort Lauderdale, Florida.

Eugenia Lamar Farrie-Henry
A Devout Mother

Eugenia (Jeanie) was born February 16, 1917 in Sumner, Georgia. She currently lives in Sylvester, Georgia. At the time of this writing, she is one hundred years old. She is the youngest child of the eleven children born to the late Turner and Josie Lamar. She is the only living sibling. When her mother died, she was about six years old. She recalls that her sister Margaret and others assisted in taking care of her.

Eugenia was always a good student in school, and she really excelled in reading, arithmetic, and many other subjects.

Eugenia began her Christian walk at an early age. She joined Miller's Chapel AME Church where she became the Missionary's secretary and treasurer and assisted with the communion service. Today her service has decreased, except to sing and read. She shared with the writer that she prays three times a day, and she gives the Lord thanks every day. Her belief is to treat everybody right.

Her first marriage was to the late George Farrie, Sr. on September 24, 1938, for about forty-five years. They were blessed with fifteen children – eight boys and seven girls: George, Lawrence, Benjamin, Charlie, Aldrin, Lewis, Marcus, Juanita, Betty,

Loretta, and Cynthia. Four children are deceased: Carrie Mae, Melva, Otis, and Annette. She has some precious grandchildren, great grandchildren, and great, great grandchildren.

Eugenia was always a homebound person and a devoted mother. Her children were trained to say their prayers before going to bed at night, and she made sure that all of them were fed.

When Eugenia was younger, she worked a little in the fields. She also made preserves, made quilts and all kinds of clothes. Gardening and baking were joyful hobbies.

Currently, she is alert and has a great memory. She can say her alphabets forward and backward. She remembers some of her children's telephone numbers without looking in a book. Guess what? She remembers the dates of her children's birth.

Eugenia's children and their families, the Matthews nieces, and all her family and friends give thanks to God for her longevity. Her family had a great celebration for her one hundredth birthday in Sylvester, Georgia.

Here is a short list of similarities of the writer and her Aunt Eugenia: (1) the writer has the same name as Eugenia; (2) the writer's first late husband was named George and her youngest son's name is George; (3) the writer's oldest son's birthday is February 16th; (4) the Lord has blessed the writer with a good memory, not as great as Eugenia's; and (5) the writer's belief is to treat everybody right and do no evil.

Shirley Matthews Plowden
A Loving Mother-in-Law

At the time I began writing this book, Shirley had shared information with me about herself. She was delighted that I was including her name in this book. I regret that I discontinued writing for a while and did not complete it before she departed this life on June 18, 2015.

Shirley was the seventh child of the late Grady and Georgia Matthews. She grew up as a child who enjoyed reading. She was an outstanding speller. When she was in junior high school, she won a spelling contest. She earned a Bachelor of Arts degree in Library Science. She worked for many years as a professional librarian and classroom teacher, in addition to other careers.

Shirley married the late, Emery Hamilton who excelled in the military. They had three brilliant, athletic sons who all have highly skilled jobs. Her sons' names are Timothy, Emery, and Sean. Each is a husband and father. Timothy is married to Jackie. Emery's wife's name is Maxine; and Sean is married to Regina.

Shirley loved her daughters-in-law and treated them as though they were her own children. Their relationship reminds me of Naomi and Ruth's relationship. Shirley was never a selfish person. She supported her children, her grandchildren, her sisters and brothers, her nephews and nieces, and her friends in whatever way she could. She even shared her home or place of residence with kindred on many occasions.

In the Book of Ruth (in the Holy Bible), it tells us about Naomi and Ruth's relationship. Naomi's husband died and later her two sons died. Her two sons' wives were name Orpah and Ruth who were from Moab. Naomi left with her two daughters-in-law to return to the land of Judah. Naomi tried to encourage them to return to their mother's house. Finally, Orpah left, but Ruth did not. She followed Naomi who eventually came to Bethlehem. Naomi's husband had a wealthy relative whose name was Boaz.

Ruth conversed with her mother-in-law about her daily encounters, especially after she met Boaz. Naomi instructed Ruth as a mother would. Boaz married Ruth and they had a son named Obed. Naomi took the child and began to be a nurse to him. "Obed begot Jesse and Jesse begat David."(Ruth 4:22)

When Shirley married Luke Plowden, she gained more children and grandchildren. She showed love to them all. During her marriage to Luke, they did a lot of traveling around the nation. They were married for about thirty-three years until his death on September 18, 2010.

As Shirley began her new life as a widow, her sons and their wives gave much attention to her needs. Shirley's relationship with the Lord gave her strength and joy. Shirley was always a blessed woman. She had immeasurable faith. Whatever she endeavored to do, she accomplished it. She decided to change careers, so she went back to school and completed that task. One time she left her beautiful home and moved to another city, but soon after that she had another one.

Shirley was always a churchgoer, but when the time was right, the Lord opened her eyes to the truth concerning the word of God. The Lord diverted her to attend Living Faith World Ministries in Daytona Beach, Florida where Dr. Tony Barhoo was the pastor. She shared with me that she attended Bible study, a prayer hour, women's ministry and much more. Her love for reading, working with puzzles, patronizing cultural activities never stopped.

Shirley was richly blessed in knowing that it was well with her soul—baptized with the Holy Ghost. This was revealed to the writer and to Shirley before she transitioned to Heaven.

Victoria Anderson
A Committed Mother

Vickie, as we call her, is the daughter of Robert and Ernestine Anderson. She was born in Sarasota, Florida, but now resides in Orlando, Florida. Vickie is best known for her hardworking spirit, knowing that she will succeed in whatsoever she endeavors to do. Nothing in her life deterred her from furthering her education beyond high school.

I'm sure Vickie wanted to set an example for her children. In addition, the more money she makes the better she could educate her children. I have always known her to have at least two jobs.

After she enrolled in college, she was hired as my secretary. She was on time, dependable, and resourceful. I could rely on Vickie to aid me in completing projects and assignments as well as her routine responsibilities. She earned an Associate's Degree while working fulltime. Later, she earned her Bachelor of Arts degree.

Vickie previously worked for the Florida Department of Children and Family Services for fourteen years. She opened her own tax company known a Quality Tax and More.

Vickie was a cheerleader from age nine years old through high school—cheering for Sarasota Ringling Reds Football League, and for the all star traveling teams for Sarasota High School. She enjoys sharing her experiences, and teaching girls and her daughter, not only to be great cheerleaders, but to be positive role models, and grow lifetime friendships.

Vickie has a passion for cheerleading. Therefore, she has been a dedicated cheerleading coach for over eighteen years starting with Sarasota Ringling Redskins as a junior coach and later as an assistant coach. She was a head coach for eight years with the Pop Warner Pine Hills Trojans.

In 2012, Vickie was offered a great challenge and opportunity with Lake Nona Junior Lions where she served as assistant coach for three years. As a coach, she won a national title in 2013. The previous year, she won first runner up.

With the help of Almighty God, Vickie was determined that her children would be successful, so she supported her son, and still supports her daughter. In every facet of their lives, Vickie's children could count on their mother to be there, regardless of the distance or the problems that occur. Vickie is a very proud mother of both her children, and she only wants the best for them.

Vickie is the mother of my grandson whose name is Marquis. Beginning as a little boy through high school, his mother found the time to involve him in many activities such as Bible School, playing basketball, singing solos, singing in the choir, playing football, participating in live jazz performances, and so forth.

After her son graduated from Booker High School, he became a student and played cornerback with the Crimson Tide football team. In fact, he was a member of the 2009 Alabama National Championship Football Team. After Marquis graduated from the University of Alabama, he was drafted into the NFL and played for the Rams for two years. Additionally, he played with the New Orleans Saints during the 2012 pre-season.

Vickie has a daughter named Skyya who is still attending University High School in Orlando, Florida. Skyya is a UHS Color Guard Band member, A National Honor Society member, an honor roll student, a member of AVID and Cougar Crazies Clubs, captain of the UHS Royal Elites Dance team, and UHS Winter Guard member. Skyya has been a cheerleader since age five, and she participates in praise dancing at church and at the Step One Dance Studio.

Chapter Six
Behaviors to Avoid

"A woman is the full circle.
Within her is the power to create,
nurture and transform."
—Diane Mariechild

Chapter Six
Behaviors to Avoid

Our behavior can sometimes influence the behavior of others, so we should practice keeping the commandments of the Lord and setting a positive example for others to follow because we know that some women are like mocking birds — don't have original ideas. Whatever some says or does, they will do the same so let us learn what is right.

Vashti

The Book of Esther (in the Holy Bible) tells us about a queen who disobeyed her husband, King Ahasuerus. Vashti's husband made a feast in Shushan the palace. Many were invited to the feast. Vashti also made a feast for the women in the house which belonged to King Ahasuerus. The king was merry with wine and he wanted to show the people his wife's beauty. Then he commanded his chamberlains to bring Vashti, the queen, to the feast. The king became very angry because Vashti refused to come.

The king asked the wise men what shall be done to Vashti because she had not performed the commandment given to the chamberlains by the king. Memucan answered before the king and the princes, "Vashti the queen hath not done wrong to the king only, but also to all the princes, and to all the people that are in all provinces of King Ahasuerus. For this deed of the queen shall come abroad unto all women, so that they shall despise their husbands in their eyes, when it shall be reported, the King Ahasuerus commanded Vashti, the queen to be brought in before him, but she came not." (Esther 1:16-17)

"Likewise, shall the ladies of Persia and Media say this day unto all the king's princes, which have heard of the deed of the queen. Thus, shall there arise too much contempt and wrath." (Esther 1: 18)

Queen Vashti's punishment was that she could not come before King Ahasuerus anymore, and her royal estate was given to another who was better than she. The king would make a decree that all wives honor their husbands.

There was a Jew whose name was Mordecai. He took his uncle's daughter, Esther and raised her as his own. Her mother and father were dead. Esther was fair and beautiful, and she was highly favored above all the virgins. Esther was chosen queen instead of Vashti.

Zeresh

Zeresh was the wife of Haman, and she encouraged her husband to wrongfully make gallows to hang Mordecai. Mordecai uncovered a plot which was to kill King Ahasuerus. Haman was promoted by the king, but Mordecai did not bow and give reverence to Haman, then he became angry. Haman planned to kill all the Jews, yet in the end, he was hanged in the gallows the way he had plotted to hang Mordecai.

Potiphar's Wife

"But I say unto you, that whosoever looketh on a woman to lust after her hath committed adultery with her already in his heart." (Saint Matthew 5:28)

Potiphar was an officer of Pharaoh, his captain of the guard. He was Joseph's master in Egypt. Joseph was made overseer in Egypt. Then he began to have problems with Potiphar's wife. "And it came to pass after these things that his master's wife cast her eyes upon Joseph; and she said, lie with me." (Genesis 39:7)

Joseph did not yield to her command. He explained to her how he had been blessed by her husband, and that he could not do this wickedness. Joseph's resistance did not stop her persistence. On another day when she asked Joseph to lie with her, he left his garment in her hand, then he got out of her way. Now she saw an opportunity to tell a lie about him. She made up a story that Joseph had tried to lie with her, and when she cried with a loud voice, he fled and left his garment.

Joseph's master put him in prison because of the lie his wife told him. The Lord blessed Joseph while in prison. Pharaoh set Joseph over all the land of Egypt. Joseph was a man of God, so regardless to how the devil tried to destroy, it came to naught. Satan uses women in so many ways to bring down people, especially men.

Jezebel

Jezebel was the daughter of Ethbaal, king of Tyre and Sidon. She was also the wife of Ahab, the son of Amri who reigned as king over Israel. Jezebel was an evil, wicked queen who had no compassion or mercy. She worshipped idols.

Jezebel tried to control her husband. She influenced Ahab to give Baal equal place with God. Also, she encouraged Ahab to oppose the worship of the Lord, destroy His altars, and kill His prophets. "When Jezebel cut off the prophets of the Lord, that Obadiah took a hundred prophets and hid them by fifty in a cave and fed them with bread and water." (I Kings 18:4)

Jezebel had the prophets of Baal to eat at her table—four hundred and fifty, and our hundred prophets of the graves. She had the audacity to threaten to kill the prophet, Elijah. He fled from her to save his life. "Touch not mine anointed, and do my prophets no harm." (I Chronicles 16:22)

Jezebel committed another cruel and wicked act when she had Naboth killed. When Naboth refused to give her husband his vineyard in exchange for a better deal, she plotted to kill him. She accused Naboth of blaspheming God and the king; so two men of the children of Belial witnessed against Naboth. "Then they carried him forth out of the city and stoned him with stones, that he died." (I Kings 21: 13)

Elijah, the prophet, prophesied about Jezebel's death: "The dogs shall eat Jezebel by the wall of Jezreel." (I Kings 21:23) This prophecy was fulfilled. "Be not deceived; God is not mocked: for whatsoever a man soweth, that shall he also reap." (Galatians 6:7)

Herodias

Herodias is a woman who retaliated in a heinous way. "Vengeance is mine, I will repay saith the Lord." (Romans 12:19) She was the daughter of Aritobulus, and the granddaughter of Herod, the Great. "But Herod, the tetrarch, being reproved by John, the Baptist, for Herodias his brother Philip's wife, and for all the evils which Herod had done, added yet this above all that, he shut up John in prison." (Saint Luke 3:19-20)

47

Herodias was angry enough to kill John, the Baptist because he made it clear that it was unlawful for her to be married to her husband's brother. However, Herod knew John, the Baptist was a just, holy man.

An opportunity came for Herodias to further express her hostility. Herod had a birthday and had a supper. Salome, Herodias's daughter danced and pleased Herod. "And he sware unto her, whatsoever thou shalt ask of me, I will give it to thee, unto the half of my kingdom." (Saint Mark 6:23). The king's oath had to be carried out. The head of John, the Baptist was given to the damsel on a charger, and she gave it to her mother, Herodias.

Delilah

Delilah was a woman who betrayed her husband for money. "For the love of money is the root of all evil: which while some coveted after, they have erred from the faith, and pierced themselves through with many sorrows." (I Timothy 6:10)

Samson love and married a Philistine woman whose name was Delilah. The leaders of the Philistines wanted to know how Samson got his strength. Everyone offered Delilah eleven hundred pieces of silver. Then Delilah began to question Samson about his strength. Samson tricked her three times. However, that didn't stop her. Delilah became relentless, using her soothing words, until Samson became so irritated that he told her the truth. He had been a Nazarite from his mother's womb and no razor had been upon his head, and if he was shaven, he would lose his strength and become weak.

His deceitful wife put him to sleep then called a man to cut off his seven locks. Then he was bound and put in prison, and they put his eyes out. When Samson's hair grew back, he used his strength to kill all those who were making mockery of him, which were thousands. He pushed down the pillars that supported the house. He asked the Lord to let him die with the Philistines.

Unfulfillment gives the devil time to work with the mind. If people would spend more time with the Lord, the mind would not stay focused on the things of the world, that which is carnal. If your mind stays on worldly things, you are a worldly person, not a spiritual person.

The Lord hates those who sow discard among the brethren and refuse to change. He that soweth discord is a traitor to the Holy Spirit. It is an abomination.

In reference to hearing/listening, lend your ear to that which is holy, and to that which is profitable unto you. Garbage belongs in the garbage. Vain babblers, news carriers, avoid. This behavior leads to unholiness.

"Now I beseech you, brethren, mark them which cause divisions, and offenses contrary to the doctrine which ye have learned; and avoid them." (Romans 16:17)

Chapter Seven
Women of Good Works

"Every wise woman buildeth her house: but the foolish plucketh it down with her own hands."
(Proverbs 14:1)

Chapter Seven
Women of Good Works

It is so important for women to exemplify intelligence and wisdom because so many females, young and old, are looking for positive role models. An intelligent and wise woman stays vigilant at all times. The Bible speaks about many women who have these attributes. Also, I know and have known personally some women with good works, but I don't have space to name them all, so the following is a list of a few.

Tabitha

Tabitha, which by interpretation is called Dorcus had her life restored unto her because of good deeds, and she gave alms such as the coats and garments that she made. Dorcus got sick and died. The saints and widows sent for Peter, and Peter kneeled down and prayed. When Peter said, Tabitha arise, she opened her eyes, and when she saw Peter, she sat up.

Pilate's Wife

Pilate's wife was a woman who warned her husband. In many situations, men don't like to listen to their wives, but in this case, she did the right thing.

Jesus was about to be sentenced to death. Pilate knew that they had delivered Jesus unto him because of envy. "When he was set down on the judgment seat, his wife sent unto him saying, 'Have nothing to do with that just man: for I have suffered many things this day in a dream because of him.'" (Matthew 27: 19)

Pilate didn't listen to his wife because Jesus was crucified instead of Barabbas who was a notable prisoner.

Abigail

She was married to Nabal, then became David's wife because of her wise decision. Nabal was a man who had great possessions. Abigail was a woman of good understanding, and of a beautiful countenance: But the man was churlish and evil in his doings; and he was of the house of Caleb. David sent his servants to ask Nabal for help, but Nabal refused. But a young man told Abigail how Nabal railed on David's servants.

David's men had been good to Nabal by protecting his sheep. Abigail got in a hurry and took bread, sheep, wine, raisins, and food and drink to take to David and his servants, but she didn't tell her husband.

When Abigail saw David, she bowed before him and gave him reverence. She begged David not to shed blood. She asked for forgiveness for herself.

David said to Abigail, "Blessed be the Lord God of Israel, which sent thee this day to meet me: And blessed be thy advice, and blessed be thou, which hast kept me this day from coming to shed blood, and from avenging myself with mine own hand." (I Samuel 25:32-33)

A few days later, Nabal died and when David heard of it, he married Abigail. Her good deeds impressed King David.

Rahab

Rahab was a harlot who demonstrated good works and that she believed in God. She was a woman who was concerned about her family not being destroyed. She opened the door for two men to lodge at her house in Jericho. Rahab knew these were men of God because of the things the Lord had done for Israel. When the men of the city came to her house looking for the men, she told them she did not know where they were. She had hidden them on her roof.

Rahab was wise enough to tell the spies this "Now therefore, I pray you, swear unto me by the Lord, since I have showed you kindness, that ye will also show kindness unto my father's house, and give me a true token: and that ye will save alive my father, and my mother, and my brethren, and my sisters, and all that they have and deliver our lives from death." (Joshua 2:12-13). Rahab had to promise that she would not tell their business, so she told the two men how to escape. The city of Jericho was destroyed and all that was in the city, except the harlot Rahab and her family because she hid the spies of the Lord.

Esther

Esther is a woman who did great, courageous deeds to save her people from death. She is also called Hadassah. When Esther's father and mother died, Mordecai, Esther's cousin, took her as his own daughter.

She became the queen of the Persian king, Ahasuerus. When two of the king's chamberlains had plotted to kill him, and it was known to Esther, she used wisdom and gave the word to her husband, and when the king found out, the chamberlains were hanged.

Haman was the son of Hammedatha, and the prime minister of King Ahasuerus. He had been promoted by the king. The servants bowed down to him, but Mordecai did not reverence him. Haman became very angry, and he made plans to destroy all the Jews — both old and young, including women and children. He received the king's consent to do this.

Esther heard about it, then she dressed in a beautiful garment and the king found favor and he permitted her to come to him. She used her intelligence to prepare a banquet to invite only the king and Haman.

King Ahasuerus asked Queen Esther what was her petition. She answered, "If I have found favor in thy sight, O King, and if it please the king, let my life be given me at my petition, and my people at my request: for we are sold, I and my people to be destroyed to be slain, and to perish. But if we had been sold for bondmen and bondwomen, I had held my tongue, although the enemy could not countervail the king's damage." (Esther 7:3-4)

The king wanted to know who is it that planned to destroy the Jews. Esther told him that wicked Haman has these plans. The king was angry, and Haman was hung on the gallows that he had prepared for Mordecai. King Ahasuerus gave Esther Haman's house, and she placed Mordecai over everything.

The king held out his golden scepter and allowed Esther to present another petition: "Let it be written to reverse the letters devised by Haman which he wrote to destroy the Jews which are in all the king's province. How can I endure to see the destruction of my kindred?" (Esther 8:5-6)

The Jews smote their enemies. Esther was granted another request that Haman's ten sons be hanged so the king ordered it to be done.

Because of Esther's obedience, she was favored by the king, and as a result, her people, the Jews were spared from death.

Fredi Sears Brown

Mrs. Brown was the only daughter of three children born to Mary Miller and Oscar C. Sears, Sr. She was born in Bradenton, Florida. She had a spiritual upbringing, a fear of God. Her father was a deacon and a founding member of Saint Mary Church, where Mrs. Brown is a current member.

Mrs. Brown was married to Ernest Brown for fifty-five years until his death in 2001. They had four children: Ernest, Kevin, Peter, and Beverly.

After graduating from college, Mrs. Brown moved to Kansas City, Missouri where she landed the post of assistant advertising manager with the black-owned newspaper. She and her husband became pioneers for the community when they moved to Detroit, Michigan.

It was in Detroit where she counselled teenaged substance abusers and prepared them for the GED test at the Salvation Army's Harbor Lighthouse. She taught English to incarcerated women at the Louise Groom's Business College, and taught preschoolers at the Unity Church.

Mrs. Brown was born during the time of segregation, so she knows what it means to be deprived of various opportunities when you are qualified. Therefore, she has a special compassion for the disadvantaged, yet her love for all mankind is seen in the work she has done.

In 1974, the Browns moved to Bradenton. I have personally known Mrs. Brown since 1978. She was my boss for a while at Manatee Community College (SCF). We worked as field recruiters for the occupational and technical programs. Her efforts to help others was an inspiration to me.

Mrs. Brown became the Manatee Community College Equal Access/Equal Opportunity Officer, and she was also an instructor. She initiated and established future, unlimited scholarships for minority students; created community-based study centers, and much more.

After Mrs. Brown retired in 1989, she and her husband used their wisdom and knowledge to educate people of all cultures. They became founders of the Family Heritage House Museum at the SCF Bradenton campus where people are exposed to many performances and activities.

Mrs. Brown has received many awards such as the 2001 Distinguished Alumni Award from the University of South Florida; Service to Youth and

Community Education Award from Links, Inc.; and Passing the Torch Award from Delta Sigma Theta Sorority, Incorporated.

Mrs. Brown knows she does not need the praise of man, but she is thankful to know that through her incredible empathy, wisdom and understanding, many have been richly blessed.

Chapter Eight
Spiritual Gifts

"A man's gift maketh room for him, and bringeth him before great men." (Proverbs 18:16)

Chapter Eight
Spiritual Gifts

The Lord said to me, "Many want gifts, but their heart must be pure. You must suffer for my namesake. You must earn gifts. Self-exaltation is not my way."

"Now concerning spiritual gifts, brethren, I would not have you ignorant. Now there are diversities of gifts, but the same Spirit. And there are differences of administrations, but the same Lord. And there are diversities of operations, but it is the same God which worketh all in all." (I Corinthians 12;1-10)

These are gifts given by the Spirit that should be used in the church by those whom the Lord chooses (I Corinthians 12:28-30): (1) apostles; (2) prophets; (3) teachers; (4) miracles; (5) gifts of healing; (6) helpers; (7) governments; (8) diversities of tongues; and (9) interpretation of tongues.

Other gifts include (I Corinthians 12: 8-10): the word of wisdom; the word of knowledge; faith; and discerning the spirits.

God's Prophetess

"Follow after charity and desire spiritual gifts, but rather that ye may prophesy. He that prophesieth edifieth the church." (I Corinthians 14: 1, 4)

A prophetess is a female mouth piece for God. Prophecy means foretelling the future and giving messages. A prophetess anointed by God will only speak what the Lord tells her to speak. If the Lord doesn't say when something will happen, it might take two days, ten years, or longer before it comes to pass. We can't be too quick to judge and call them a false prophetess.

A woman should be anointed by God in order to become a prophetess. We can so easily exalt ourselves. The Lord gives prophecy in so many ways such as in dreams, in visions, in verbal conversations, and in many other ways. You might have a dream as a child and the dream is realized, but that does not mean you have the gift of prophesying — interpreting the word of the Lord.

It is important that a prophetess warn the people, tell them what thus saith the Lord. If you don't, their blood is at your hands. On the other hand, if you obey, you have delivered your own soul. Don't worry about being rejected, just OBEY the Lord. Sometimes people in high places need the help of prophetess. Someone who has a close relationship with God. There is a warning from the Lord for those who prophesy: "Woe unto the prophets that prophecy lies. Woe unto the prophets who prophecy for shekels. Woe unto the prophets who rob my people. Woe unto the prophets who go their own way and who say, this is my synagogue — allowing the house of God to be polluted because it is their synagogue."

A warning to the people who disbelieve God's prophetess and fight against them. The Lord says, "Touch not my anointed and do my prophets no harm." (Psalm 105: 15) The Lord revealeth his secrets unto His servants, the prophets. (Read Amos 3:7)

All through the Old and New Testament, and in today's world, many messages were given about many things: many prophets spoke about the coming of Jesus Christ, the Messiah, even after He was born. Suppose the Lord had not spoken to Joseph when King Herod tried to kill Jesus. Joseph was warned, and he obeyed.

Old Testament Prophetesses

Miriam was the daughter of Amram and Jochebed, her mother. Her brothers were named Aaron and Moses. When Moses was a baby and placed in the river, Miriam stood afar off to see what would happen to him. She asked Pharaoh's daughter should she call a nurse of the Hebrew women to nurse the baby. "And Miriam, the prophetess, the sister of Aaron, took a timbrel in her hand; and all the women went out after her with timbrels and with dances." (Exodus 15:20)

Miriam and the women were rejoicing because of the miracle through her brothers—the horse of his rider drowned in the Red Sea, and Israel was brought safely across the sea.

After Israel came forth out of Egypt, Miriam was stricken with leprosy. She and Aaron spoke against Moses, their brother. This was done because he had married an Ethiopian woman. However, God had mercy when Moses cried unto the God to heal her. She was healed after she was shut out from the camp seven days. The journey through the wilderness resumed after Miriam was brought forth again. "When the children of Israel abode in Kadesh, Miriam died there, and was buried there." (Numbers 20:1)

Huldah was a prophetess whose husband was named Shallum. She lived in Jerusalem during the time Josiah reigned as king. During this time, the Book of the Law was found in the house of the Lord by Hilkiah, the high priest. The people had not hearkened unto the words of this book. The king told Hilkiah and others to enquire of the Lord for him, and for the people, and for all Judah because the Lord's anger is against them. So Hilkiah the priest and others went unto Huldah, the prophetess.

Huldah's prophecy, "Thus saith the Lord, God of Israel, tell the man that sent you to me. Thus saith the Lord, behold, I will bring evil upon this place, and upon the inhabitants thereof, even all the words of the book which the king of Judah hath read:

"Because they have forsaken me, and have burned incense unto other gods, that they might provoke me to anger with all the works of their hands; therefore, my wrath shall be kindled against this place, and shall not be quenched." (II Kings 22: 15-17)

The prophetess prophesied that King Josiah has humbled himself, and the Lord has heard his cry, so he will die in peace and his eyes will not see the evil He will send upon Jerusalem.

"And **Deborah,** a prophetess, the wife of Lapidoth, she judged Israel at that time they were oppressed." (Judges 4:4). Deborah assisted Barak in delivering Israel.

Israel had been oppressed into the hand of Jabin, King of Canaan. The captain of Jabin's army was Sisera. Deborah judged Israel at that time. The children of Israel came up to her for judgment.

Deborah talked with Barak about taking ten thousand men to subdue the captain of Jabin's army. Barak said he would go if she went with him.

Then Deborah prophesied: "For the Lord shall sell Sisera into the hand of a woman." (Judges 4:9) Barak went after Sisera. "Sisera fled away on his feet to the tent of Jael, the wife of Heber, the Kenite." (Judges 4: 17)

Sisera came to Jael's house and asked for water. Jael gave him milk to drink instead of water. He fell asleep and Jael took a nail and hammer and smote Sisera into his temples. Deborah's prophesy was fulfilled—Sisera died. Israel prospered after Jabin, the King of Canaan was destroyed. Deborah and Barak sang a song of praise.

New Testament Prophetess

Anna was a prophetess who blessed Jesus when he was presented as a baby in the temple. "And there was one Anna, a prophetess, the daughter of Phanuel, of the tribe of Aser; she was a great age and had lived with a husband for seven years from her virginity: and she was a widow of about fourscore and four years, which departed not from the temple, but served God with fasting and prayers night and day." (Saint Luke 2:36-37)

Philip, the evangelist, had four daughters who were virgins and they did prophesy. (Acts 21: 9)

Hedy Lee Floyd
A Woman of Many Gifts
(Deceased 1994)

Sister Floyd was a woman whom I knew for many years. She was also called Mother Floyd. She was indeed a prophetess, a healer, a preacher, a teacher, a piano player, and singer. She ministered in music for many local churches. She was a woman of many gifts.

Mother Floyd was born in Stark, Florida to Ella Louise and Alexander Smith. At the age of one year old, her family moved to Plant City, Florida where she spent her childhood. She met and married the late Reverend J. H. Floyd and relocated to Sarasota, Florida.

Many years ago, Mother Floyd gave me this testimony about herself and I quote: "From a child I have known the voice of the Lord, and I had seen things come to pass that He spoke to me. I was raised up in a small city by my mother who was a devout Baptist Christian.

I could always tell her my visions and she would give me her interpretation and guidance. I found out before my mother died that she slipped down to a holiness church and received the baptism of the Holy Ghost. Years after her passing, I would still have these strange visions and had no one to share them.

Having been married to a Baptist minister for twenty-four years, and being indoctrinated in the Baptist faith, I always knew there was more that met the eye, so I began to seek the truth about the Holy Ghost. After my husband died, I was alone and had more time to search. After reading Galatians 5:16-17, Hebrews 10:26, Acts 19:1-12 and I John 3:8, I realized I was not in fellowship with God; therefore, I prayed and asked God to give me what I needed to get into the kingdom.

One month later, in my beauty parlor, I received the baptism of the Holy Ghost and the gifts of the Spirit. I had the anointing to heal and miracles were performed immediately. Since that time, I accepted my calling into the ministry which had taken place years ago. Today, I am happy being saved and working for the Lord until the day He says welcome home."

Mother Floyd did so much for many people, but I have a personal testimony about the messages and prophecies she gave me. She said that the Lord told her I was a nobleman. I didn't want to believe that because I remembered the scripture that says, "For ye see your calling, brethren, how that not many wise men after the flesh, not many mighty, not many noble, are called." (I Corinthians 1:26)

Mother Floyd also told me that I had the gift of inner healing, and that I was using the gift already. I didn't know I had the gift until she explained how the gift is used. The Lord told Sister Floyd on September 11, 1991 that I was a spiritual attorney for God.

I do know that every battle that infringed on my life, I had the victory. One time, I acted as my own attorney in court. There were many more confirmations regarding the words spoken by the prophetess.

On September 9, 1982, Mother Floyd spoke in
tongues and said that I had the gift of the power of
prayer, a gift which includes praying for offerings,
and for special requests or needs that a person might
have. There is much more that I cannot explain at this
time.

Sarah Matthews Greene
Gift of Helping

Sarah is the youngest of the seven daughters
whom Grady and Georgia Matthews raised. She is a
sister of the author. The Lord has blessed her to be
able to help others. Many people who can help others
don't.

Since her childhood, Sarah was compelled to go
to church. On Sundays she attended services all day
long. Currently, she and her husband James reside in
Ocala, Florida, and are members of New Covenant
Missionary Baptist Church. She is a member of the
deaconess ministry; chairs the Black and White
Banquet and Awards committee; serves on the
culinary committee and is the director of Sunday
School.

Sarah does more spiritual work in her
community. Evidently, she has read the scripture that
says, "It is more blessed to give than to receive."
(Acts 20:35) There are so many ways you can help
and give to others; serve as a taxicab driver, or loan a

car; visit the sick; support financial dilemmas; give advice on multiple issues; feed the hungry, the disabled, the rich and poor; give gifts to uplift; and much more. Sarah has done all these things.

To further explain, she is a great cook, so in order to bring the family together and fellowship, she invites the family to her home for a Thanksgiving meal — enough food to feed a whole community.

Sarah gives this help to her son and grandchildren, to her sisters, to her nephews and nieces, to her in-laws, to church members, and to many more.

Sarah's work history and awards are so extensive that I will mention only a few. She is a consultant, motivational speaker, and trainer for community action and head start programs throughout the country. She began to work independently on a part-time basis on January 1, 2015. While serving in this capacity, she is a CAA/Head Start advocate at various association events.

Prior to January 1, 2015, she worked as vice president of Business Initiatives for Application Link, Incorporated. She assumed this position March 17, 2015. In this capacity she was primarily responsible for creating and establishing a National Head Start Alumni. She used her knowledge and experience to help Application Link, Inc. advance its goal of helping administrators of Head Start and community based organizations operate more efficiently and effectively through the intelligent application of new business technologies.

Before this, Sarah was the President and CEO of the National Head Start Association for almost 17 years. In that role, she supervised office operations, acted as ambassador and advocate for the Head Start community and provided insight for the future direction of the organization.

Sarah was regularly invited to the White House to testify before Congress and meet with federal officials. She participated in national forums that set policy and direction for the early care community and served as the spokesperson through a variety of media outlets including major newspapers, magazines, and national television such as NBC's Today Show with Matt Lauer, BET, CNN, C-SPAN, Dateline, Time, and Delta Sky Magazine.

Sarah currently serves on the Board of Directors for the local Marion County Head Start agency, Child Development Services, Inc., branch secretary of the Marion County NAACP, co-chair for the former Belleview Santos High School Reunion committee, and a member of the Head Start Scholastic, Inc. as well as Health Connection, Inc. advisory boards. She is also the treasurer of Mu Alpha chapter of Zeta Phi Beta Sorority, Inc.

"Give, and it shall be given unto you; good measure, pressed down, and shaken together, and running over, shall men give into your bosom. For with the same measure that ye mete withal, it shall be measured to you again." (Saint Luke 6:38)

Chapter Nine
Teachers of Righteousness

"And He gave some apostles;
and some, prophets; and some,
evangelists; and some pastors
and teachers; For the perfecting
of the saints, for the work of the
ministry, for the edifying of the
body of Christ."
(Ephesians 4:11-12)

Chapter Nine
Teachers of Righteousness

A teacher is one who gives instruction; imparts knowledge to help others learn. There are all kinds of teachers, but a teacher of righteousness is a gift from God. Some women are afraid to accept the gift of teaching in fear of being rejected, or they think this gift is only given to men.

Titus 2:3-5 tells us that "The aged women likewise, that they be in behavior as becometh holiness, not false accusers, not given to much wine, teachers of good things; that they may teach the young women to be sober, to love their husbands, to love their children, to be discreet, chaste keepers at home, good, obedient to their own husbands, that the word of God be not blasphemed."

I have observed and experienced that some young women don't want the aged women to teach them face to face, instead they want to be the older women's supervisor or boss, and at the same time, learn from them without mentioning their name.

I have often called myself an "unidentified teacher". This is a good thing because there are different ways to teach. I observed a long time ago that whatever I do or say, others will repeat it, but don't mention my name. This would often happen in my church, on my job, and in other settings.

74

For example, one time I gave a young lady a message from the Lord to give to her child. Some weeks later, this mother was preaching at a church, and her subject was the same message I gave her to give to her child. The mother didn't expect me to be at the service.

Another way to teach is to be an example for others to follow. If you teach thou shalt not steal, you don't want others to see you stealing. When our children watch what we do and hear what we say from the time of their birth, we are teaching them.

We must receive the baptism of the Holy Ghost, before we become a teacher of righteousness. Learning God's word should be a daily duty. Oftentimes, we get so anxious to teach others when we have not learned the word. So many times, I have said, "The more I study the word of God, the more I realize how much I don't know.

Remember, you don't have to study the word for thirty years before the Lord blesses you with the gift of teaching. "For when the time ye ought to be teachers, ye have need that one teach you again which be the first principles of the oracles of God; and are become such as have need of milk and not of strong meat. For everyone that useth milk is unskillful in the word of righteousness: for he is a babe." (Hebrews 5:12-14)

Do's and Don'ts

DO have knowledge of the subject you teach. "Study to shew thyself approved unto God, a workman that needeth not to be ashamed, rightly dividing the word of truth." (2 Timothy 2:15)

DON'T be a false or bad teacher. "For there are many unruly and vain talkers and deceivers, specially they of the circumcision: whose mouths must be stopped, who subvert whole houses, teaching things which they ought not, for filthy lucre's sake." (Titus 1:10-11)

DON'T add or take away from the word of God. "For I testify unto every man that heareth the words of the prophesy of this book. If any man shall add unto these things, God shall add unto him the plagues that are written in this book; and if any man shall take away from the words of the book of this prophecy, God shall take away his part out of the book of life, and out of the holy city, and from the things which are written in this book." (Revelations 22:18-19)

DON'T think that you know it all. Be teachable — not lifted up. "For I say, through the grace given unto me, to every man that is among you, not to think of himself more highly than he ought to think; but to think soberly, according as God hath dealt to every man the measure of faith." (Romans 12:3)

DON'T ask questions or give assignments to students unless you know the answer.

DON'T abuse your position.
A fool knows when he/she is being targeted. There is a difference when one is teaching the pure word, and when one is slinging mud.

DO be alert and sober; for slicksters will come to test or challenge you. "And, behold, one came and said unto him, Good Master, what good thing shall I do, that I may have eternal life? And He said unto him, why callest thou me good? There is none good but one, that is, God: but if thou wilt enter into life, keep the commandments." (Saint Matthew 19:16-17)

DO live what you teach.
"Thou therefore which teachest another, teaches thou not thyself? (Romans 2:21) Don't be a hypocrite like the Pharisees, the Sadducees, and others.

If God has blessed a woman to become a teacher of righteousness, she should use every opportunity to teach the women about the "saints" apparel, a debatable/controversial topic. I believe that too much emphasis is placed on the outer appearance, instead of focusing on circumcising the heart. We can dress in white and look like saints, but still have a dark heart.

However, if you are "not" a saint, there are no restrictions on how you dress. On May 15, 2008, the Lord said, "Man sets dress code for himself, but I have a standard for those who live a holy life. Why should women wear pants and that's the dress for men? Would you want to see a man wear a dress or skirt?

As a part of Moses' law, "The woman shall not wear that which pertaineth unto a man, neither shall a man put on a woman's garment: for all that do so are an abomination unto the Lord thy God." (Deuteronomy 22:5)

In the New Testament, the Bible says, "In like manner also, that women adorn themselves in modest apparel, with shamefacedness and sobriety; not the braided hair, or gold, or pearls, or costly array; but which becometh a woman professing godliness with good works." (I Timothy 2:9-10)

If a woman has long hair, it is a glory to her: for her hair is given for a covering." (I Corinthians 11:15)

How we fix our hair is an added attraction to a woman's holy appearance. If women should wear a cover for her head and for her glory, why should men wear long hair? Why should they look alike when the Lord made them different?

Who is the greatest teacher? "And the Jews marveled saying, how knoweth this man letters, having never learned? Jesus answered them, and said, 'My doctrine is not mine, but his that sent me.'" (Saint John 7:15-16)

"But the Comforter, which is the Holy Ghost, whom the Father will send in my name, he shall teach you all things, and bring all things to your remembrance, whatsoever I have said unto you." (Saint John 14:26)

Rosa Lee Thomas
A Calling to Teach

I am a native of Sarasota, Florida, one of ten siblings of the late Elder Willie Sr. and Agnes Mayes. When I was young, my sisters and I were known as the preacher's kids; therefore, we had to be careful wherever we went.

I know God was in the plan when I married Rayford Thomas. The Lord blessed us with a lovely daughter named Melanie, and a grandson whose name is Derrek. These three people are gifts from God.

I was raised to go to church faithfully. I attended New Zion Primitive Baptist Church. All my life I knew the Lord but didn't realize the seriousness and realness of serving God. My brother, Elder Willie Mayes, Jr. is my current pastor.

When I was thirty-three years of age, I was minding my own business, so I thought, when I was attending a Sunday School class. The deacon of the church said, "Sister Thomas, I would like for you to teach the young peoples' class" which was made up of junior and high school students.

I replied, "Deacon, I just can't do it because those kinds know more than I do. They are smart kids who like to ask a lot of questions." Thankfully, the deacon would not give up on me, so I eventually consented.

The first lesson I had to teach was about Moses. Moses didn't think he was worthy to do what God had called him to do. Moses said, "I am slow of speech, and of a slow tongue... The Lord said Go, and I will be with thy mouth, and teach thee what thou shalt say." (Exodus 4: 10, 12)

"I know Aaron the Levite thy brother can speak well, and thou shalt speak unto him, and put words in his mouth: and I will be with thy mouth, and with his mouth, and will teach you what ye shall do." (Exodus 4:14-15)

This is what I said to the Lord: "Lord, you need to do for me what you did for Moses. Then I heard in my spirit, study, study, study. I had heard that very deacon often quote a scripture from 2 Timothy 2:15, "Study to show thyself approved unto God, a workman that needeth not to be ashamed, rightly dividing the word of truth." I know I could not escape what God was calling me to do.

When the time came, I stood before the class to teach, and I got so carried away in teaching the word about Moses and the children of Israel. I knew more than I thought I knew. They had to ring the bell for me to stop. It was time for class to end. I've been teaching ever since.

I love the word of God. It is food for my soul and strength for my body. There were seventeen kids I taught and some of them became preachers, teachers, administrators, and had many other careers. The students have come back to thank me for the teachings they received. I have even taught some of their children. God is good!

Another confirmation of my calling was in the 1970's. I used to sit under the teaching of an elderly Bible missionary whose name is Sister Doll Dean. She would use so many parables when she taught scripture. Some were very funny to me because she made things rhyme. For example, she would say, "Keep on sinning, you got enough meat on your bones to pay for it."

She would also say, "Your mouth is not a river, but it will sure drown you." Then she shared a conversation from Saint John 21 when Jesus asked Peter if He loved Him. She reminded me that Peter said, "Yeah, Lord; thou knowest that I love thee. Jesus said, Feed my lambs. Then He asked Peter the same questions and told him to feed my sheep, feed my sheep."

This is a saying that I have always heard and did not know what it meant, so I asked my mother what it meant. My mother explained the scripture to me. I knew that the Lord had a work for me to do. He had souls, young and old, for me to teach. God also told me to counsel.

A minister named Bishop Porter said that the Lord has work for me to do; and that I could do all things through Christ which strengthens me. I took heed and continued in my calling and allowed the Lord to lead me. I was once slain in the spirit and I was saying, "Lord, I will do what you want me to do, and I will go where you want me to go." Through His grace, I have kept my word.

I have been teaching in my church's school with youth and adult classes; in senior mission every week; in our association and district P.B. convention; in a seminar for one whole week in Tampa, Florida with a class of eighty-seven ladies nightly; and in other doors that have opened. My basic teaching is to "know the truth and the truth shall make you free." (Saint John 8:32)

Currently, in addition to Bible teaching, I labor for the Lord in other spiritual capacities on a national, regional, and local level. I worked over thirty-seven years in the medical/healthcare profession, and for many years I was a decorating consultant.

Chapter Ten
The Lord Will Save You

"And she [Mary] shall bring forth a son, and thou shalt call his name JESUS: for he shall save his people from their sins."
(Saint Matthew 1:21)

Chapter Ten
The Lord Will Save You

Regardless of your age, or how bad you think you have been, or what trouble you have encountered, the Lord will save you if you call on His name. It is God's will that no man perish.

There was a man named Zaccheus who was rich, and he was a publican. He wanted to see Jesus, so as Jesus passed by, he ran up a sycamore tree because he wasn't too tall.

Jesus looked up and saw him and told him to come down. He was going to abide in his house for the night. Zaccheus repented of the things he had done and was ready to rectify his wrong doing.

Jesus said to him, "This day is salvation come to this house, forasmuch as he also is a son of Abraham. For the Son of man is come to seek and to save that which was lost." (Saint Luke 19:9-10)

"For what is a man profited, if he gains the whole world, and lose his own soul?" (Saint Matthew 16:26)

During the time Paul and Silas were put in prison, they sang praises unto God. An earthquake came, and all the prison doors were opened. When the keeper of the prison awoke out of his sleep, he wanted to kill himself because he thought the prisoners had fled. Paul told him not to harm himself because they had not left.

Then the jailer fell down before Paul and Silas and said, "Sirs, what must I do to be saved?" And they responded, "Believe on the Lord, Jesus Christ, and thou shalt be saved, and thy house." (Acts 16:31)

Peter asked the Lord to save him. When Jesus was walking on the sea, his disciples were afraid. Jesus assured them that it was he, not a spirit. Peter asked if he could come to him and Jesus said, "Come". Peter came down out of the ship and began to walk on the water to go to Jesus. He began to sink but he called on Jesus. He said, Lord save me, and Jesus caught him.

In Saint Matthew 8:23-27, it tells us that Jesus had entered into a ship and his disciples followed him. While Jesus was asleep, there arose some boisterous weather in the sea. The ship was covered with the waves. Jesus' disciplines were afraid, and they woke up Jesus saying, "Lord, save us: we perish!"

Glenda Cannon
The Life of a Young Convert

We are never too young to give up the world and follow Jesus. I surrendered my life to the Lord at age nineteen, and I have not looked back. I was born April 11, 1960 to the union of Johnnie and Mary Burston. I have four brothers. My father and one brother are deceased.

As a look back over my life, I can see that the hand of the Lord was always upon me, especially since I was in some difficult situations, but God kept His protection around me.

When I was in the ninth grade in 1974, a storm was taking place in our area and the meteorologist was sending warnings. The evidence of the bad weather included the wind which was very boisterous. The sky was dark, and there was heavy rain. I was home alone, not having a relationship with God at the time, yet I prayed for protection.

During the storm I fell asleep and when I awoke, everything was calm and there was no damage to our house. I realized that God had heard my prayer. There were so many things where God had heard my prayers, and He put dreams and visions in my heart.

In 1978, I graduated from Southeast High School in Bradenton, Florida. My education was interrupted by my pregnancy and marriage, but God rescued me. In the months before my conversion, our Heavenly Father led my mother to Mount Moriah Christian Church. Sister Delores Morris invited her to attend a service. However, she soon moved into another ministry.

When I first visited Mount Moriah, Reverend Wesley Tunstall, Sr. preached and extended the invitation for those who wanted to accept Christ. My mother encouraged me to go to the alter. I obeyed my mother, but Reverend Tunstall asked, "Who sent you here?"

I replied, "My mother."

He said, "You go and sit down and make up your mind to come for yourself." He ministered to me about counting the cost. I went home and literally took a piece of paper and drew a line of what I would gain and what I would lose.

After about two weeks, I went back to church determined to forget about getting revenge and willing to lose friends, lose family and so forth. My husband and I surrendered to God at the same time in July of 1979. My husband was delivered from cigarette smoking, but he did not continue to serve the Lord at that time. However, my daughter and I continued to persevere on our journey in the Lord. Through Mother Hedy Lee Floyd, the Lord named our daughter Virginia.

I desired to know God's word for myself, so I began reading and studying day and night until God brought enlightenment. He told me to preach the gospel, His word. The Lord continued to manifest Himself to me: our daughter experienced some intestinal discomfort. A prophetic word came for me to give her Borden's milk. After I obeyed, there were no more problems.

Another blessing was when our second child was born in 1981. We named him Charles Isaiah. By being a Head Start parent, I had the opportunity to further my education. I can remember as a child about the age of ten years old, I said that I wanted to be a nurse. I received a nursing license (LPN) in 1982.

I had been a CNA for five years before becoming a nurse. And when I thought our child rearing years were over, eight years later, Aaron J. Cannon was born in 1989. The name Aaron was given from the Lord.

In 1993, things began to turn in my husband's life. He had not attended church for about twelve years, but he came back. However, seven years later, I experienced a crisis in my life. I had never been sick before other than a rare headache maybe once a year.

Suddenly, a sickness came upon my body and I experienced swelling all over. I had hair loss, weight loss, and loss of strength. I couldn't kneel down to pray. In the midst of all of this, I began to lactate as if I had just had a child. The doctors thought I had a brain tumor, so a MRI was done which came back negative.

I was sent to a specialized endocrinologist who ordered medication. I took it for a short time, but my spirit kept saying to me to step out on faith and stop taking all the different medications. Today, I no longer take any of those medications with my body being under attack by the enemies, and the suspicion of a brain tumor. My faith had to be consistent in God.

God, through His son, Jesus Christ, has worked so many miracles in my life and my husband's life. God also did miraculous works in my children's lives.

Jesus had been a lawyer in the courtroom for my son, Charles on more than one occasion. He performed financial miracles; and given salvation.

A few years after my daughter graduated from high school, she left the church. However, the training was done so she returned. Her life is like mine. She has two sons and one daughter, and the Lord is saving her husband.

Another healing in my family involved my husband. In 2013, he was having some discomfort in his back. The doctor ordered an x-ray and unbeknownst to us, they found a mass. The biopsy showed that it was cancerous. Through faith, prayers, treatments and changes in diet, God performed a miracle again!

My mother's faith in God, even while enduring the most adverse situations, has helped to anchor me. The Lord delivered her, saved her, healed her, and He made provisions for her when there was not a way or opportunity with man.

As for me and my house, we will continue to walk in faith and trust in the Lord.

Nevada Tunstall Robinson
A Dedicated Saint
(Deceased May 15, 2016)

During the time I was writing this book, Nevada left us to be with the Lord. I talked with her on the telephone the day before death came. She was very excited about me selecting her name to be in my book, so she gave me this information about herself.

How many women do you know who would drive ninety-two miles one way to attend church? Most of the time she would be the first one present for the nine thirty Sunday School service. It disturbed her when others were late. This is an example of true dedication.

Nevada, who was known by many as Aunt Nevada was the eighth child of the late Hollis and Elizabeth Tunstall. She was born in Finchburg, Alabama. She was about ten years old when her daddy died. Then the family moved back to Baldwin County in Daphne, Alabama.

She came to Auburndale, Florida in 1964 and this is where she resided until her death. She birthed and raised three children who are Beverly, Steve, and Daryl. She was a grandmother and great grandmother.

At the age of thirty-three, she decided to give up the world, meaning there would be no more marrying men and no more children. She wanted Jesus to be the only man in her life. She cried out to God for Him to help her because the life she was living wasn't worth going to hell for. This lets us know that she was not confused as to what she wanted to be in life. Her mind was made up.

She worked for Griffin County Fruit Company for twenty-five years. One Tuesday morning before she went to work, she was filled with the Holy Ghost which was March 23, 1976. Later, in that same month, the Lord told her to preach, and He gave her the gifts of healing. (All preaching is not done in the pulpit.)

Nevada also worked for the Polk County School Transportation Department from 1990 to the Friday before her death. In 1997, God told her to go to Mount Moriah Christian Church in Sarasota, Florida where her brother, the late Bishop Wesley Tunstall, Sr. was pastor. She traveled and evangelized with her brother in so many places in the state of Florida and around the country.

She was blessed as a prophetess, a teacher, and as an anointed singer, although she thought she could not sing. Two outstanding talents she had were cooking and sewing. She made lots of beautiful garments and other things for the ladies. I think everyone enjoyed her cooking, and I know it made her happy to feed the hungry. She even knew how to make candy.

Jesus spent some of his time feeding the hungry, even when his disciples wanted to send the people away. "And when it was evening, his disciples came to him, saying, this is a desert place, and the time is now past; send the multitude away, that they may go into the villages, and buy themselves victuals. But Jesus said unto the them, they need not depart; give ye them to eat." (Saint Matthew 14:15-16)

Chapter Eleven
The Beautiful Tree

"And he shall be like a tree planted by the rivers of water, that bringeth forth his fruit in his season; his leaf also shall not wither: and whatsoever he doeth shall prosper." (Psalm 1:3)

Chapter Eleven
The Beautiful Tree

Whatever career or vocation you choose, you want to become a beautiful holy tree. There are times the Bible refers to us as trees. "Either make the tree good, and his fruit good; or else make the tree corrupt, and his fruit corrupt: for the tree is known for his fruit." (Saint Matthew 12:33)

Sometime in our lives, all of us wish we could turn back the clock and erase certain decisions we made. We think we would have done things differently. If we don't make wrong choices, obviously, we will never know what is right for us. Some good advice is to seek the Lord in everything you attempt to do, whether it pertains to your spiritual life or non-spiritual life.

If God gives you an answer, OBEY Him! Women have rights today. Don't allow men to deter you from obeying God. I will expand on some of the gifts that are mentioned in chapter nine of this book.

Let us focus our minds on pastoring. A pastor is a leader, a preacher, a teacher, one who is called and anointed to be a faithful servant for the Lord. A pastor is a shepherd who watches over the flock and is responsible for the souls of the flock.

Jeremiah 3:15 says, "And I will give you pastors according to mine heart, which shall feed you with knowledge and understanding."

I have a testimony about when the Lord called me to pastor. On the first Sunday in 1995, I wore a new, white outfit to church. When I went to bed that night, I had a dream and I was wearing the same white that I had on the first Sunday. I was standing at the podium in the pulpit. The Lord spoke in a loud voice, "My daughter, I have called you to pastor."

I woke up out of the dream and fell on my belly and said, "Lord, this is the last gift I want, but I will do your will." That same morning as I was washing dishes, the Lord told me that He would send me a husband and He gave the reasons why. The same year, on November 4, 1995, Jacob and I were married.

On September 29, 2004, the Lord said, "Jeanie, I have called thee, my daughter, to be the pastor of your ministry." I am reminded of the biblical story of the elect lady. "The elder unto the elect lady and her children, whom in the truth; and not I only, but also all they that have known the truth; I rejoice greatly that I found of thy children walking in truth, as we have received a commandment from the Father." (2 John 1:1,4)

I asked the Lord to explain who was the elect lady. He said, "One who fears God, in high position with followers. You do not have to have a gorgeous temple to conduct service in. She did a spiritual work wherever she could with followers. She was commended for her work. Jeanie, you are an elect lady who has been chosen to lead others."

More instruction concerning the gift of pastoring include the house of God being governed by my Spirit. "Often leaders lift themselves up; they exalt themselves above the people. The people, the flock who are hungry and scared, have no one to turn to. The leaders have failed Me. They preach on Sunday for shekels and say, I am your pastor with no concern for the soul. However, they want shekels and they rob the poor."

"I am hungry saith the Lord of hosts. Why worry about a crowd? With a crowd, there will be more confusion. The world looks for a crowd. Pastors are looking at more money, not souls or work."

If you have been called to pastor, you must preach also. You must preach the gospel. Paul says in I Corinthians 15:3-4, "For I delivered unto you first of all that which I also received, how that Christ died for our sins according to the scriptures: And that he was buried, and that he rose again the third day according to the scriptures."

"For I am not ashamed of the gospel of Christ: for it is the power of God unto Salvation to everyone that believeth; the Jew first, and also to the Greek." (Romans 1:16)

Salvation comes through preaching of the gospel. "And how shall they preach, except they be sent? As it is written, how beautiful are the feet of them that preach the gospel of peace and bring glad tidings of good things." (Romans 10:9)

There are many who say they are preaching in the name of Jesus, but their feet are not beautiful. They are going their own pernicious ways.

On Wednesday, March 6, 1996, the Lord gave me this message: "I make my preachers. Every preacher has to go through the valley. If you don't, you will not be able to stay on the mountain—it will not stand. You can't appreciate being on top if you have not been down.

How can you properly counsel and minister to others if you have no experiences and no testimonies? Why do you think I said that every mountain shall be brought low, every crooked way made straight, every rough road made smooth, and every valley shall be made high?

Moreover, every phase of your life that shaping up, trimming…doing away with or adding to, I will make you and mold you to the preacher I want you to be, not the preacher you want to be. If you have had no trials, you will not stand.

Gold must be tried in the fire. When you become humble, and obedient, then your feet will become beautiful as you preach the gospel as I said before. Then I can send you when you're being tried by fire.

On March 25, 1997, the Lord said to me, "I have anointed thee, my daughter, to go into all the world and preach the gospel, heal the sick, raise the dead, give sight to the blind…" An apostle is one who is ordained and sent to do a specific job for the Lord.

An evangelist is a traveling preacher. He/she carries the word of God from place to place to convert the sinner to Christianity. In II Timothy 4:5, the Apostle Paul told him to make full proof of his ministry and do the work of an evangelist.

In today's world, the Lord has called many women to pastor/preach, to evangelize, to teach, and to do much more to build the kingdom of God. Many use too many excuses for what they have been called to do.

The Lord has given me messages to give to certain women regarding their calling. Some accepted the messages and obeyed, and others didn't. Some are in their graves because of disobedience. On the other hand, some exalt themselves and refuse to wait on the Lord.

You cannot make yourself great and use the name of the Lord. The Lord wants true laborers in the vineyard. In the Bible we can read about the women in the Old Testament and in the New Testament who did great works for the Lord.

Some labored with their husbands and with the Apostle Paul and with others. Priscilla was the wife of Aquila who was a tentmaker just like Paul. Priscilla and her husband traveled with Paul making disciples.

There was a man named Apollos who was very knowledgeable in the scriptures, but he only knew about the baptism of John. "And he began to speak boldly in the synagogue: whom when Aquila and Priscilla had heard, they took him unto them, and expounded unto him the way of God more perfectly." (Acts 18:26) The Apostle Paul referred to Aquila and Priscilla as "helpers in Christ Jesus." (Romans 16:3)

Phebe was another servant of the Lord: "I commend unto you Phebe our sister, which is a servant of the church which is at Cenchrea: that ye receive her in the Lord, as becometh saints, and that ye assist her in whatever business she hath need of you: for she hath been a succourer of many, and of myself also." (Romans 16:1-2)

A Samaritan woman met Jesus at the well. After holding a conversation with Jesus, she left her water pot, and went into the city and told them about a man who told her everything she did. She testified about Jesus and many of the Samaritans believed, and when they talked with Jesus, they believed for themselves.

Mary Magdalene was a woman who loved Jesus. She was a woman whom Jesus had cast out seven devils. She showed her gratitude in different ways. She had an alabaster box of very precious ointment and poured it on Jesus' head.

His disciples thought it was wasteful for her to do. Then Jesus said, "Why trouble ye the woman?

For she hath wrought a good work upon me. For in that she hath poured this ointment on my body, she did it for my burial." (Saint Matthew 26:10, 12).

After Jesus' resurrection, He appeared to Mary Magdalene and gave her a message to give to his disciples, his brethren. The woman whom some wanted to stone to death because she was caught in the act of adultery, she became a beautiful, holy tree according to Jesus' doctrine.

Chapter Twelve
Three Personal Testimonies

"And they overcame him by the blood of the Lamb, and by the word of their testimony; and they loved not their lives unto death." (Revelation 12:11)

Chapter Twelve
Three Personal Testimonies of Faith

Vivian Matthews Brown
A Survivor

"I, Vivian, am the tenth child born to Grady and Georgia Lamar Matthews. Presently, there are four of the thirteen children remaining which include myself. I was raised in a very strict home environment that involved many chores such as raking yards, washing clothes by hand, cleaning the house, ironing clothes, working in watermelon and tomato fields, cooking meals, washing dishes, babysitting, and so forth. Whippings were the main form of discipline which was common in that era of the past.

As a child, I enjoyed listening to stories told by my sister Jeanie and playing naughty tricks on her. Also, my siblings and I were often taken to the lake to swim during the summer months. Holidays were wonderful in those days. We decorated a Christmas tree, and had toys the best our parents could afford.

My mother made sure there were new shoes and outfits for Easter. We colored eggs and enjoyed Easter egg hunts given by the church, at home, or at school. There was lots of baking sweets and other food, not only at Thanksgiving, but during the week day and every Sunday after church service.

Attendance at Stanton First Baptist Church was a must for Sunday school, worship service, BYPU, and night service. I believe my father enjoyed listening to me sing "Standing in the Judgment We Got to be Tried." I sang this song when I was a teenager in the church choir.

I taught myself how to sew as a young child. I would find old clothes and sometimes new cloth to cut out patterns on newspaper, then I would sew them by hand. My mother would have me sew her slips or whatever was needed. She would tip me, maybe a dime, which was very welcomed at that time.

I was known for my high school scholastic ability. A small scholarship was awarded to me as a result of scoring the second highest on the state test at my school, Belleview-Santos High. Thereafter, I began attending junior college in Ocala, Florida.

I transferred to Florida A and M University in Tallahassee, Florida in order to earn my Bachelor of Science degree. My educational goals were eventually accomplished at Bethune Cookman College in 1976 at Daytona Beach, Florida. The extended time span I spent out of school was due to dropping out for a long period of time as well as financial difficulties, immaturity, marriage, and other events. On the other hand, the success of my life that I am most proud of is my four daughters.

My firstborn, Corendis is an award-winning educator who has served in public schools for almost 30 years. She is also a writer and business owner. She is the proud mother of my first grandchild, Felicia.

Cindy is also a successful educator. She is married and a devoted mother of two children, Logan and Nia.

Tiffany, my third child, serves as a teacher, too. She is engaged to be married. She works for Chicago Public Schools.

Aleatha, my youngest daughter is a nationally certified school psychologist. She is married with one son, Ian. She is also a certified fitness instructor.

My retirement from the state of Florida which was more than thirty years occurred during the end of December in 2008. It is a blessing to have retired successfully after years of working with children and their families, the court system, and law enforcement.

In view of this chapter of my life, I have always been very blessed by the Lord, my Savior. God has brought me through poor judgment of thinking, adverse decisions for companionship, and He has allowed me to live despite medical issues.

I cannot thank and praise our Heavenly Father enough for bringing me through seen and unseen dangers. I am eternally grateful that He continues to do this each and every day.

Presently, my strong desire is to please the Lord, enjoy family and friends, and life in general—

this is the delight of my heart. I attend and participate in worship service at Mount Mission Church where I sing in the senior women's choir. I am also involved in other missions such as Bible study, prayer groups, and so forth."

Luvenia Mayes Gibson
A Woman of Faith and Courage

Luvenia is the oldest child of the late, Reverend Willie Mayes Sr. and Agnes. She is a native of Sarasota, Florida. She and her husband, John Henry reside in North Port, Florida.

The experiences that Luvenia shared with me, convinced me that in addition to her faith, she has strength and courage. She was raised in a Christian home and she knows the power of prayer.

From the age of seven years old, she suffered with headaches. She would become blind, and the light and noise made her head hurt worse. Sometimes, she would even become unconscious. About every three months this would happen. Her daddy would drive her to the doctor's office. She didn't work anymore, so she began to ask the Lord to take her out of this world. Her parents were grieving.

One day she called her daddy to the bed and asked him to go and get Elder Ford and his people to come and pray for her. Later, three ladies came singing "My God is Able to Do All Things". After they left, she sat on the side of the bed by herself. She was healed!

The doctor had told her parents that she would not live beyond twelve years old. However, she was twelve when the Lord healed her.

She got married at a young age to Handy Jacob Wooten, Sr. (He is now deceased.) He was a handsome, brilliant, and church-going singer. Before the public, he was friendly and nice, but at home, he was a different man who was mean and abusive. He had problems when he left the military. A teenager can easily be deceived.

Luvenia became the mother of nine children. Five are still alive. Their names are: Handy Jacob, Jr., Marcia, Kathy, Gerald, and Stanley. She also has several grandchildren and greatgrandchildren.

Luvenia shared that her children's father became her worse nightmare for over ten years. He would beat her for everything that displeased him. For example, if the food burned, if all the wrinkles were not out of the clothes that she ironed or if she left the house or had friends.

Finally, she threatened him. She told him what she would do if his behavior didn't stop. Later, she hit him in the head with a hot skillet. He quickly left the house after that happened.

When her children's father was home, he kept food in the house, but now she didn't have the finances to support her five children properly.

However, during a time of desperation, Luvenia's father would bring over a bag of groceries. Also, her eldest son would share his earnings with his mother when he cleaned old ladies' houses, and when he worked for his granddaddy or when he went into the military and set up an allotment for his mother.

Luvenia had the fortitude to upgrade her skills, so she enrolled in night school to get her high school diploma. She did domestic work during the day to earn money. She eventually graduated from school by having persistence, faith and with prayer.

Another great thing that happened in Luvenia's life was when she got employed at Sarasota Memorial Hospital, and later with the Health Department. She continued to work in the health profession until she retired.

While she was in nursing school at the hospital, she had some health issues that involved her kidneys. One whole kidney had to be removed. During the time of the surgery, she was thinking about the Lord and praising Him for His goodness and mercy.

In the meantime, the doctor had signed the documentation for the removal of her body to be taken to the morgue. She heard everything that this man had said, and she was at peace. Then the door to her room was opened and a nurse saw that she was alive, so she ran and told the entire staff what she saw.

The Lord had brought her spirit back into her body. This reminded me of what the Lord said to me on September 28, 1999: "I breathe breath into man and I can take breath away from man. I can perform any miracle that I choose. I am God and besides me, there is none other."

Jesus performed miracles in the Bible. In Matthew's gospel, a ruler named Jairus had faith that Jesus could raise his daughter from the dead. Jesus took her by the hand, and the maid arose. That same power is here on Earth today!

Bernice Wilson Randall
A Dependable Servant

Bernice is a woman you can depend on. Whatever she says she is going to do, you can count on it! She is faithful and on time for any occasion. She goes the extra mile to aid people in need.

Bernice shared an interesting story about her early childhood through her adult life. She said, "I am the oldest daughter of nine children born to the late Woodrow and Ophelia Wilson of Ailey, Georgia.

At an early age, I knew the Lord was drawing me to Him. When I was about eight years old, I would sit and rock my sisters and brothers in my lap and tell the Lord I don't want to be bad.

Our family church was named Saint Mary Baptist. As a teenager, this church is where I taught Sunday School and Bible class, yet I loved to attend the Holiness Church. I, along, with my brothers and sisters, and the neighbors' children, would walk to Sunday School which was about a mile or more.

Our parents were strict about us being late, so there would be elderly ladies and deacons who would tell our parents if our behavior wasn't good.

I was raised up working on a farm. My parents raised me to work hard. They said if I didn't work, I would steal and go to jail, so I thank God that me nor my siblings went to jail for stealing.

After moving to Sarasota, Florida, I had three jobs: cleaning banks at night, sewing at a garment factory, and working at National Linen Company which is now called ALSCO. I retired after working forty-two years. I can now dedicate more time to the work of the Lord.

I am the mother of one child whose name is Jason. I knew after becoming a mother, I would have to become that role model that God wanted me to be. I had given my life to the Lord, but I was searching for more.

In Sarasota, I became affiliated with different churches. I was trying to find the truth. I don't regret giving my life to Jesus because He's been everything to me. I must confess that there were times I wanted to give up, but I couldn't. The Lord kept me when others wanted to destroy me.

Time after time, I would see this particular lady and I didn't know her name, but I was drawn to her. Every time I would see her, I had to talk to her. Finally, Pastor Wooten invited me to her Bible study and that was about eleven years ago.

As I began to increase in the knowledge of God, and be filled with the Holy Ghost, joy filled my heart in spite of my trials and tribulations. I thank God for letting me know Pastor Jeanie Wooten. It has truly been a blessing! She is a woman who can get a prayer through; a mighty woman of God who is my spiritual mother."

Jeanie Matthews Wooten
My Path to Success

"Work hard in silence. Let
success be your noise."
—Author Unknown

Jeanie Matthews Wooten
My Path to Success

I am the eighth child of Grady and Georgia Lamar Matthews who were descendants of slaves. On April 21, 2001, the Lord said to me, "You were the chosen one to lead thy people out of bondage."

Throughout this book, I have made references about myself in several chapters. Chapter Five explains how I was raised when you read about mothers. I have included this chapter to encourage all readers not to doubt what they are capable of doing.

If you want to become a journalist, an evangelist, a military officer, a maid, a teacher, an attorney, a singer, or whatever, it may be. Don't underestimate yourself. Find yourself.

I made an "A" in an art class when I was in my early thirties. Until then, I had always told myself that I could not draw a straight line with a ruler. I will continue to reiterate that we search the scripture to find ourselves spiritually. Let the word of God apply to us.

Your definition of success might be different from mine. Nevertheless, here are a few of my accomplishments, both spiritual and nonspiritual that I praise God for. I knew at a young age that without the Lord, I could do nothing.

*Earned ribbons and medals in track and field events.

*Voted to be Miss Stanton Junior High School. I rode on a float in a parade.

*Won a dancing contest as a teenager, having a partner. I borrowed my sister Georgia's green skirt.

*Worked as an usher in church and led songs in the choir beginning at age six or seven.

*As a teenager, organized Christmas programs for children.

*Captain of the girls' basketball team at Stanton Jr. High, Belleview-Santos High School, and Hampton Junior College.

*President of my junior and senior class.

*Valedictorian of my senior class. I had to write my own speech and memorize it with the help of a supervisor.

*Met Jesus Christ for the first time and accepted Him as my personal savior on November 10, 1976. Prior to this experience, I was just a church-goer.

*In 1977, I was introduced to the miracle-working power of God. He miraculously healed my painful knee. There have been more healings since then.

*Preached my first sermon on July 30, 1978 from Isaiah, chapter six. I memorized the entire chapter.

*Given my first song from the Lord in 1981 entitled, "I'm Nobody Lord". Many songs have been given since this time.

*Anointed to be a prophetess on Tuesday, September 7, 1993.

*During the 1970's, I led songs with my choir that were recorded on an album while attending Mount Herman AME Church in Fort Lauderdale, Florida.

*Played my first song on the piano in 1996. It was "Oh How I Love Jesus". I am self-taught.

*Worked as a chairperson, with the aid of my daughter and son for a Matthews, Mathis 3-Day Family Reunion. Over two hundred kindred came from various states including New York, Michigan, Texas, Georgia, Florida and more.

*Worked as a chairperson for a Lamar Banquet in 2004. Over eighty people attended.

*Author of my first book in 2008. The Lord told me that he had given me the spirit of writing like he gave the Apostle Paul.

This was a confirmation of what my disabled sister, Pearl had said to me in 1994. As I sat in my bed and was writing, Pearl stood at my bedroom door and asked, "Jeanie, who gave you the spirit of writing?"

In 2008, the Lord told me to organize a group of singers entitled, "Jeanie Wooten and the Anointed Voices."

I retired from my career as an educator in 1993. Presently, I am pastoring, evangelizing, preaching, teaching, singing, songwriting, prophesizing, praying and much more with the help of my husband, Jacob.

Jacob and I spend as much time as possible with our children, Epkins, Jeana, Jerome, George, Lawanda, Nathan, and Leshia, and their families. Our seed is blessed. The Lord has given them intelligent minds and professional jobs. Our grandchildren and greatgrandchildren are doing well, also.

Thank you for purchasing and reading this book. I pray that you were blessed and that it draws you closer to God. Feel free to contact me using the following information:

Wooten Ministries
2400 Walker Circle
Sarasota, Florida 34234
Phone: (941) 366-2943

Ministers Jacob and Jeanie Wooten

Notes

Notes

www.ingramcontent.com/pod-product-compliance
Lightning Source LLC
Chambersburg PA
CBHW021931040426
42448CB00008B/1013